The Life of the Virgin Mary

St Maximos the Confessor

Patristic Theology

St. George Monastery
Anna Skoubourdis
Monaxi Agapi

Published by: Virgin Mary of Australia and Oceania 2020 ©

oceanitissa@gmail.com
www.oceanitissa.com.au
Youtube: Oceanitissa

Translated by Timothy Fisher

Subscribe to receive updates and Orthodox Christian creative media

www.oceanitissa.com

The Life of our Most Blessed Lady, the Theotokos, the Eternal Virgin Mary:

A Brief Exposition of her pure and blessed life, from her birth to her dormition, written by our blessed Father Maximos the Philosopher and Confessor

I: THE CHOSEN FRUIT OF OUR RACE AS AN OFFERING TO GOD

Hear this, all peoples (Ps. 48:1), and give ear, all inhabitants of the earth. Come, all you faithful and gather, all you who love God, kings of the world and all peoples, rulers and judges of the earth, young men and young women, elders and children, every tongue and every soul! Come to honor, praise and glorify the most holy and pure, the most blessed eternal Virgin Mary, the Mother of Christ our God, who sits enthroned in royalty above the Cherubim and the Seraphim, within the city of God, which basks so radiantly in His glory (Ps. 86:3); the one chosen before all the ages according to the mysterious design of God (cf. Eph. 1:4-5);

the temple of the Holy Spirit,
the wellspring of living water,
the garden of the tree of life;
the beautiful and fruitful vineyard
from which runs the stream of immortality;
the river of living water,
the ark that contained the Uncontainable;
the golden receptacle of the manna of immortality,
the unsown stalk on which grew the grain of life,
the flower of virginity, replete with fragrance and grace,
the lily of divine beauty,
the Virgin and Mother who bore

the lamb of God who takes away the sin of the world (cf. Jn. 1:29),

the upper room of our salvation
the most highly exalted of all heavenly powers.

All you peoples who have received the proclamation of the Gospel, lift up your hands and sing praise to her with joy and with sweet words; let your voice be heard, let it resound, for this is our duty; let every tongue and every human nature sing glory and praise to her, from whom our salvation came!

But how did this come to be? God, the Creator of all things, had to find a worthy and pure dwelling place of divine beauty in order to come among men; and such was this blessed and venerated Virgin. *The King considered her beauty* (Ps. 44:1) and saw fit to dwell in her. In the same way it is now our duty to sing her praises, that we may be given a worthy tongue and such sharpness of thought to express her glory and adoration as we ought. But no man could sing and glorify the holy Theotokos as divinely as she deserves; even if ten thousand tongues were gathered, even if all the nations of men were joined together, they would not be enough for the blessedness of her glory and praises. Therefore, since we can never give her the glory of which she is worthy, we will demonstrate the fiery love that drives us to praise and sing to the Mother of God, our hope and mediator to God, as best we know how. Thus, just as no strength is sufficient to glorify her beloved Son and God, so also the strength of our words of celebration which we intend to dedicate to his most Holy Mother, her gentle mercy will judge with favor, for she knows our weakness and yet she still loves us.

We will proceed to discuss (with the grace and succor of the most holy Theotokos), the circumstances of her birth and who her parents were, her upbringing and her immaculate ways, what praise her honor garnered and was a credit to her entire life, from her birth until her dormition, since it is her grace and succor that gives us strength and fitting words and moves our tongues. Moreover we should not be remiss to say a few words about her Lord and God, such as is in our power, since all her radiance and majesty emanates from Him who is the very glory and beauty of his immaculate Mother.

Furthermore, we ought to confirm that everything we shall write and reveal is sure and trustworthy, for it comes from reliable witnesses, from the congregation of those who love God. Using the holy evangelists and Apostles as our primary foundation, we will proceed to the holy and inspired Fathers, whose words are full of all wisdom, written by the grace of the Holy Spirit, and whose deeds are lovely and pleasing to God. These are Gregory the Wonderworker of Neocaesarea, Athanasius the Great of Alexandrea, the blessed Gregory of Nyssa and Dionysus the Areopagite, together with their fellows in sanctity and concord. Should we include anything from the Apocrypha, that will also be true and free of falsehood, having already been accepted by the holy Fathers we have mentioned. As a matter of fact, St Gregory of Nyssa says in one of his homilies: "As I have read in an apocryphal book, there was something noteworthy about her conduct as regards the law, and the father of the most holy Virgin Mary was renowned for his kindness."

His name was Joachim, of the house of David, the king and prophet; his wife was named Anna. Joachim had remained childless even into old age, for his wife was barren. Nevertheless, by the Law of Moses she was accorded equal honor with the women who had born children, such as no childless woman had ever been given. For Joachim and Anne were exceedingly pious and thus were held high regard in both word and deed; they were also well known, for they came from the line of Judah and David and were descendants of the kings. As we know, the houses of Judah and Levi had united, and thus the priesthood was comingled with the royalty. This had been written in fact not only about Joachim, but also about Joseph, to whom the holy Virgin was betrothed. And although the Gospel records only that the one side, the more direct side, was *of the house and kindred of David* (Mt 1:20; cf. Lk 2:4), in fact both were equal heirs; of David by nature, of the Levites by law. It further mentions that the blessed Anna was a chosen scion of the same tribe, which shows that the King that would be born of her daughter would be the great high priest as well, since He was the God-man. In any case, the venerable and esteemed parents of the Virgin were deeply grieved because they had no children, for foolish people heaped abuse on them, since according to the Law of Moses they were not permitted to offer their gifts in the Temple; and they sought a means of having children not only to remove the reproach from themselves, but from the whole world as well, and to bring forth glory from on high. Then the blessed Anna remembered Anna the elder, the mother of Samuel (cf. 1 Sam 1:9), and took refuge in the temple, entreating the Creator of all things to bring forth fruit from her womb, so that she in turn could dedicate to Him the gift that He would give her. Joachim likewise busied himself with entreating God to deliver them from their infertility.

The merciful and generous King granted the righteous man's prayer and sent good news to them both separately. He announced it to Joachim first: as he was standing in the Temple praying, he heard a voice from on high saying, "You will have a child that will be glory not only for you, but for all the world." Joachim recounted this same annunciation to the blessed Anna, but she did not cease praying to God with hot tears. A little later God sent a message to her as well as she was in the garden making entreaties and supplications to God. The angel of God appeared before her and said, "God has granted your prayer; you will give birth to the bearer of joyful news and will call her Mary, from whom will come the salvation of all the world." A short while after this joyful annunciation, the barren Anna conceived and gave birth to Mary, the one who gives light to all; for that is the meaning of the name Mary – the Light-bearer.

Then the honored parents of the blessed and holy child were overjoyed, and Joachim organized a feast, to which they invited all the neighbors, the wise and the simple. All of them praised God, who had done such a spectacular miracle in their midst by turning Anna's sorrow into indescribable joy and thanksgiving, and that she had been found worthy to be the gateway of the gateway of God, the door of life and the beginning of his glorious plan for salvation.

We must now exalt the quality of our speech to the glorious and highest mysteries of the child of God, by her grace, intercession and help; for she is the ground and benefactor of every good thing.

When she was weaned – she who would give milk to Christ our God for our sake, who would be born of her – and was three years old, her blessed parents brought her to the Temple of God and presented her as a dedication to God, with all appropriate praise and honor, as they had promised Him before her birth. Many virgins went before her and led the way with burning torches, just as the prophet and king, the forefather of the immaculate Virgin, had foretold, *Maidens will be taken away in her train to the king, those near her will be taken away to you* (Ps 44:15). The prince of prophets had in fact thus foretold her consecration in the temple by the virgins, some of whom went before her and some of whom followed after.

Of course, this prophecy does not only concern those maidens, but also all virgin souls thereafter who follow in her footsteps; this is why he calls them 'those near her'. And even though all fall far short of loving her as they should and imitating her, still, by her Grace and goodness that flow from the Lord and her son, these souls of the saints were called 'near her', just as the Lord and Maker of all things Himself deigned to call those who were pleasing to Him and walked in His ways His brothers. So it is true that all the souls of the righteous ones, who through their holy lives are given the grace to love her, will be joined by grace to her Lord and Son and be taken into the celestial Holy of Holies. In the same way her Son entered the Holy of Holies *as our forerunner* (Heb 6:20; 9:12), as the Apostle Paul says; so also she, the most holy Mother of the Lord, will enter first of all into the heavenly rest, and then the rest of the souls of the saints will be led in after by virtue of her intercession.

I am compelled to mention the later deeds of the Virgin of heavenly beauty, but my spirit cannot compete with the words of the blessed prophet David. So we shall begin a little before and examine which prophecy bound the glorious king and prophet together with his blessed queen and daughter, the Mother of God. In fact, in the forty-fourth Psalm he mentions her King and Son, when he says that the Holy Spirit imparted to her His glorious attributes: His beauty, both spiritual and physical, the outpouring of grace over her lips and the bestowal of wisdom, the anointing with the oil of gladness, the arrows of power, the protection of the bow, the sword strapped around His waist, and the royal scepter (cf. Ps. 44:2-8). All of these are a proclamation and a pattern of His incarnation, which truly did bring about peace and righteousness, and above all else His dominion over all the world, His victory and His eternal kingdom. Now, he applied these grand prophecies to the person of our Lord Jesus Christ, and he used them to adorn His most blessed mother. And even though some commentators have applied these epithets to the Church, that does not hinder us in the least from applying them to the holy Mother of God as well. For the words of the Holy Spirit should not be taken in just one way, but in various related interpretations, since they are a treasure trove of many good things; this is why the Fathers who applied them to the Church spoke correctly. But it would also be true and accurate to examine the prophecy and see that it belongs to the Mother of God as well.

So you see how sublime its teaching is, not only in regards to entering the temple, but also all her other spiritual gifts and her beauty: *The queen is at your right side* (Ps. 44:10). This passage refers to her presentation and entry into the Temple, how she took her place to the right of the ark in the Holy of Holies, which truly is the 'right side' of God. And then it describes all the array of her adornment, meaning the beauty of her finery: *All the glory of the king's daughter within, clothed in golden tassels, resplendent* (Ps. 44:14). It means here the raiment of her soul which is full of God's graces; in fact, everything it says refers to her spiritual attire, including when it speaks of her golden apparel, all her various adornments, it first means that they are sublime and celestial in their own right, and their grace is all the deeper and richer when they are gathered together and united, since they have all been concentrated within the blessed soul of the utterly spotless Virgin. This is why it says 'clothed' and 'resplendent', meaning a loveliness made of good deeds and holy words, in perfect harmony with her God and Savior. And just as the rainbow that shines in the clouds is one in essence and name, and yet has many colors and a pleasing appearance, thus also the immaculate Virgin grew inexpressible adornments of beauty from her earliest youth, all with distinct shades of color; and when she had grown to maturity, thus also blossomed the beauty of her adornment. This is why *the King desired her beauty* and came to dwell within her.

How good and profound are these words: *Listen, daughter and see and incline your ear* (Ps. 44:11). 'Listen' to what the Holy Spirit proclaimed in ages past concerning you, just like what has now happened to your parents, their barrenness and extreme old age, their prayers and petitions, the annunciations from God, and, by His grace, your miraculous and fully unexpected birth. 'And see' how you enter into the temple and take up your reverent abode behind the inmost curtain, and how you now miraculously dwell within the Holy of Holies; for only the high priests enter there *once a year* (Heb. 9:7). 'See' your wondrous dwelling and the even more wondrous Benefactor of your dwelling, 'incline your ear' and prepare to receive the good news, the glorious annunciation and immaculate conception of the Word of God. And may your mind not return to your people the Jews and to your father's house. *Forget your people and your father's house*, as well as every earthly thing, and clothe yourself with a new mind and a firm hope, and thus *the King will desire your beauty* and you will be truly worthy to be called His mother. But he rendered this relative prophecy even richer and foretold that the wealthy would be sent to serve her. Thus he says, *the wealthy of the nation will entreat your face* (Ps. 44:13). Even then many noble and chosen people from the nation had gathered at her entrance into the temple, but also now the wealthy, meaning those who are filled with divine grace, serve her and glorify her in the Holy Spirit. Therefore, in order to demonstrate that her outward deeds were a reflection of her inward deeds, and that her deeper and more glorious inner majesty might shine through her outward piety, it says: *All the glory of the King's daughter is within* (Ps. 44:14). It goes on to describe her inner riches not only by her consenting to God's design, but also by her display of the gifts of the Holy Spirit deep within her heart, so numerous and lovely that they defy description. This host of riches caused her to accept the golden garment, *clothed in golden tassels, resplendent* (Ps. 44:14). Therefore just as the external beauties are taken severally according to the attributes and are then brought back together to compose her raiment and her colorful adornment, in the same way the graces and the rest of the inner adornment which indwells the blessed Virgin are also distinct and have been prepared and brought to her by the Holy Spirit Himself.

And so the Virgin was presented at the Temple, where so many wonders occurred that my frail spirit cannot give form to it, nor can my earthborn tongue lend it expression. How then did she live in the Temple and what wondrous scale of virtues did she ascend? We must ourselves climb this heavenly ladder in thought, for when she took up the new and marvelous mission and entered the Holy of Holies, her conduct there became difficult to see, and she grew even more miraculous. Her spirit deepened further, and she received her food from heaven, from the very archangel's hand. As she grew and matured physically, so also her spirit was honed and enriched, and the angel who sustained her instructed her in all integrity. In the words of Luke the Evangelist concerning her Son, He *grew in grace and stature*, meaning He flourished more and more in the grace of the Holy Trinity. So also, she progressed in physical stature according to the sustenance she received from her provider, and in spiritual discernment according to her exalted instructor, who had been given to her by the grace of God as her special guardian. This was the state of affairs for the one who had been chosen to contain the uncontainable divine nature in her womb, what a supernatural miracle!

For these reasons the Scripture speaks of her physical form and characteristics, since everything about her was wondrous, exceptional, and glorious. Since she loved learning, she had great acumen and retained every good word within her mind. Her inmost being was already absorbed in study and contemplation of the holy Scriptures and all wisdom, since she was to become the Mother of the Word and Wisdom of God, mighty in word and discernment, as it is written, the Lord *opened her mouth carefully and lawfully, and she created order with her tongue* (Prov. 29:43). Solomon carries on about her in the same vein: "*She has clothed herself with strength and dignity* (Prov. 29:42), meaning the Grace and Power to which she gave birth. She clothed herself with power and dignity from Him who became flesh within her. Thus the rest of the passage also applies to her: *And she rejoiced in the last days* as Queen of all things, for she contains all things and everything from one end of the earth to the other bows to her and renders her praise, for she reigns together with her Son and Lord, and she will reign all the more 'in the last days', when this fleeting world draws to a close. Then she will reign with her dearest Son in His kingdom that abides for all time and defies description.

It is indeed appropriate for us to appeal to those passages of Scripture that most aptly describe her and complement each other's meaning. Many women have amassed spiritual and material riches; *many daughters have acquired wealth, many have attained power, but You surpass and outstrip them all*, both physically and spiritually, and you are 'greater' than all of them by the divine grace of your miraculous child.

While these testimonies from Scripture have somewhat delayed our telling the story of her life, it is still good and fitting that they be cited, for they have been written for her glory and the benefit of those who love God. But now let us return to the purpose of this work; truly, just as the Mother of God is exalted above all compare and her glory surpasses all others, so also her spiritual labor and her very way of life are unparalleled. In the eyes of everyone she was a vessel positively filled with grace; I will even go further – she was beyond all grace, awe-inspiring, full of understanding in appearance and conversation, seer of the visions of God, a stranger to all distress, wrath, and indecency, beautiful in body and soul, graceful and upright, and abounding in all adornment and every virtue. She was indeed by nature such a holy virgin that it did not bother her in the slightest when suffering came upon her and tried to disturb the purity of her soul.

So her holy soul was rich in love and compassion towards others and thus in grace and mercy more like her Son than any other; peaceful and humble in thought, exalted in abundant virtues and boundless grace. She is truly the Queen over all creation in word and thought and deed, for she was to become the mother of the true King of all the world, who became poor and humbled himself for our sake *unto death, even death on a cross* (Phil. 2:8). In the same way, the blessed and exalted eternal Virgin was poor and humble of heart and spirit, as in the Lord's beatitude. She submitted herself to the priests and honored their wishes; she was revered by all, for she had been born by divine grace and would give birth to the King of men and angels. Thus the power of God overshadowed her from earliest childhood and adorned her, body and soul, with every manner of goodness like a golden tapestry of countless colors. This was her rank and form when she entered the Holy of Holies as the true holy offering and spiritual image, the paragon of reason, the terror of demons and desire of angels. I will go even further: Wondrous and terrible even to the angels, but pleasing and obedient to the Father and the Son and the Holy Spirit.

This is why even the blessed David and the other prophets of old proclaimed her to be the *mountain of God, a goodly mountain, a mountain rich like cheese* [...] *the mountain upon which God has seen fit to dwell* (Ps. 67:16-17), the city of God, surrounded by lofty words (cf. Ps. 86:3), *holy ark in which the Lord rests* (cf. Ps. 131:8) and *Zion*, which *the Lord has chosen and ordained to be His dwelling place* (Ps. 131:13). She, they said, is the throne of God (cf. Is. 6:1; Dan. 7:9), the chariot leading thousands of the angelic hosts (*the chariot of God is a thousand-fold* [Ps. 67:18]) in unspeakable brilliance; the forbidden garden, the spring of living water (cf. Song 4:12, 15), the scroll sealed shut of which the ancient books teach, on which the unwritten Word was written, with no beginning and no end; the royal bed over which the 'sixty mighty men' (Song 3:7) stand guard, who are the words of the holy Scriptures that teach about her; the holy lampstand, the royal scepter which sprouted miraculous buds, the vessel bearing the manna from heaven, the table of the bread of life, the tablets of the true Law, the ark, *gilded on every side* (Heb. 9:2-4), meaning with the grace of the Holy Spirit; the one who bore the uncontainable Lord of all creation.

So the most blessed Virgin dwelt in the temple in stillness (cf. Ps. 45:11) and dedication, with an orderly life and pleasing to God, and grew more in stature and excellence of virtue than in knowledge. And who could fully describe her pains and prayers, enriched with every good work? She had already displayed as much from her youth, and so all her doings were unfathomable to everyone else, and her whole life was likewise wondrous, for she had been chosen to be the Queen of all things and mother of the King and Lord and God of all; thus she had been ordained by the Father and prepared by the Holy Spirit to bear within her the only-begotten Son, who is inseparable from them, the Word of God, in her womb, and to be the occasion of His incarnation and dwelling among men. And while, as I said, it would be a colossal and unrealistic task to enumerate all the marvels of the time she spent there and the deeds that she did even as a young girl in the temple, I will at least mention the most impressive gift she received during all her countless labors and petitions.

After she had been there for several years, when she had just turned twelve, there came a sign that was herald and forerunner of the gospel. She was full of all wisdom and righteousness and spent her life in fasting, prayer, humility, and the love and fear of God. One night, around midnight, as she was offering prayers and petitions to God with a contrite and pure heart in the Holy of Holies, behold! A wondrous and fearsome thing occurred; a bright light shone within the sanctuary, so brilliant that the light of the sun is like a shadow beside it. And a voice rang out from the altar, saying, "Mary, you will give birth to My Son!" When Mary heard this, she was not startled or frightened, although she was still a child, still less was she proud or overly joyful; she told it to none of the others and did not change her behavior or thoughts in the slightest, but she was taken aback at the way the prophecy had been announced. So she hid this deep in her heart, the tremendous mystery, ordained before time itself began, concealed even from the angels, until the wonder of the God's plan of salvation should be fulfilled through her and she give birth to the Lord Christ. Then the purpose of His sojourn among men would be accomplished, and he would rise from the dead and ascend into heaven.

The holy Virgin continued to grow and eventually turned fifteen, at which age it was customary to marry under their law. Nevertheless, the priests were reluctant to give her up, since they were afraid to send the one who had been consecrated to God away from the temple, and it was an awful thing for them to hand over God's sacrifice to be married; for He had ordained her to be His bride alone. But on the other hand, the Law of Moses forbade a young woman to remain in the temple permanently after she had come of age. Caught between these two conflicting necessities, they convened a great council to decide on the best course of action. The Lord then put a clever and fitting suggestion in their hearts, how they could comply with the Law's stipulation while still avoiding the marriage; they decided not to wed her, but only to betroth her to some man who was too old and decrepit to consummate the marriage, yet who was faithful to keep her virtue in pledge, so that he might even become the protector of her virginity. (This was also a part of God's great plan.) For just as the Lord and King of all things Himself hid the blinding light of His divinity in shrouds of flesh, that the prince of darkness might not recognize Him, so also by His mother's virginity remained concealed under this outward betrothal. This was so that no one could guess how and when she had conceived, and thus could she thwart the faithless enemy who knew from the words of Isaiah and the other Prophets that the Deliverer would come into the world from a virgin.

While the priests all came to this conclusion, they dared not take any righteous man's gifts as pledge, but entrusted everything to the providence of God, just as Moses had done of old, when many were seeking the office of high priest. Although he did take pledges for the office, he left the decision to God. He placed the staves of the twelve tribes in the Sanctuary and discerned from the way one of the staves blossomed the will of God (cf. Num. 17:8). And again in latter days, Peter and the other Apostles prayed and cast lots and so found the one who should take the traitor's place. So also here the priests began to pray and seek the Lord under the guidance of the great Zachariah, father of John the Baptist, on whom rested the grace of the high priest's office. He had furthermore witnessed the holy life and unbelievable tenacity of the most blessed Virgin's prayers in the Holy of Holies. During the order of his course in the temple, when the matter was brought to discussion, Zachariah suggested as much for the holy Virgin; not only because she was of his same line since the royal house had joined with the priestly house, but also because she was related to his wife Elizabeth. Zachariah had learned from other records that Mary and Elizabeth were the daughters of two brothers, and this was confirmed by the word of the archangel, as is written in the holy Gospel: *and behold, Elizabeth, your relative* [...] (Lk. 1:36). So the Lord gave Zachariah an idea. He distributed twelve palm branches to the old and venerable elders who would sue for the holy Virgin's hand and laid them on the altar of the temple. He and all the other priests prayed and entreated God with earnest tears and begged him to work a miracle sufficient to show if one of them was fit to take the Virgin. The Lord gave them a great sign, and Joseph's branch blossomed and put forth shoots, just as Aaron's staff of old; and thus did Joseph take the immaculate Virgin into his care from Zachariah, by the will of divine providence and the priestly council, so that the great mystery should be born of her and she should minister to it, the miracle that surpasses all understanding.

Now this Joseph was then an elder much advanced in years, more than seventy, so that no one would harbor the slightest suspicions about the marriage. He was a widower of small substance, since the One he would take into his house and raise in the flesh would become poor for our sake, in order to make us rich by His divinity. He was a carpenter by trade, more skilled at his craft than all the other carpenters, for he would serve the true builder, the Creator and Craftsman of all things. At the same time Joseph, as famous as he was for his craftsmanship, was equally reputed for his gentleness, his piety, and his good deeds. He was the most virtuous of all the elders who were present, except for the parents of the holy Virgin. But why must we go on about Joseph, when God himself bears witness to his righteousness? Yes, Matthew the Evangelist testifies: *Now Joseph was righteous* (Mt. 1:19). So when Joseph took the holy Virgin from Zion in Jerusalem, he brought her to Galilee, to the city of Nazareth, for that was the very place of the glorious mystery which would translate us to the heavenly and invisible Jerusalem. It was here that the awesome and indescribable wonders began to take place that would draw us up to the royal throne, at the coming of the Word of God, the King and Creator of all things.

Now when Joseph brought the holy Virgin Mary home with him as queen and lady over his house, he introduced her to his children, as was written concerning Joseph the Elder: *Pharaoh made him ruler over his house and sovereign over all his wealth* (Gen. 41:40; cf. Ps. 104:21). So also did this Joseph make her mistress, overseer, and ruler over all his house. He appointed the holy Mary to be teacher of his daughters so that she would impart to them what she herself knew, that they might become wise, as the Prophet says (Ps. 104:22). Even though they were older, even still by the grace of the Holy Spirit Mary was more mature, since the blessed and most holy Virgin was truly rich in virtue; more than anything else she had attained quietness, peace, and humility. Most of the time she stayed at home, deep in prayer and petition to God, fasting and exercising her spirit. When she left the temple it was almost time for the Feast of Booths, when the ark had come to rest (cf. Gen. 5:4). It was the seventh month according to the Hebrew calendar, and as always, the High Priest Zachariah entered the Holy of Holies to burn incense before the altar. He was told of the birth of John, for the lampstand must come before the light, the dawn before the sun, the voice before the word, the friend before the Bridegroom and the shield bearer before the King. Truly the lesser miracle of the barren woman's conception must precede the greater wonder of the pure Virgin birth, as was confirmed by the word of the archangel who said, *Behold, Elizabeth your relative has also conceived a son* (Lk. 1:36).

II: THE ANNUNCIATION

Now, when six months had passed after Elizabeth's conception, the archangel Gabriel was sent from God to the city of Nazareth, to the house of Joseph, and announced to the Virgin Mary this truly good, glorious, and marvelous news, inexplicable and incomprehensible, the sum and bedrock of every good thing. But when and how and where did the annunciation take place?

The Virgin had been fasting and was standing next to a well, for she would truly give birth to the wellspring of life. It was the first month, the same in which God had created the whole world, by which He wished to show us that He was now remaking this old world afresh. It was the Lord's Day, the first day of the week, when God had once put an end to the ancient darkness and created the light before all else, when our King and the Son of God's servant would rise in glory from the grave together with our own nature; it was not only the first day, but even the first hour in accordance with the word of the Prophet: *and God will come to her aid at the break of dawn* (Ps. 45:6).

But how wondrous and mysterious were the archangel's words! *Greetings favored one* (Lk. 1:28); 'Greetings' was said to remove that age-old grief and calamity of the Fall, as well as to indicate the new grace of knowing God that is now given to mankind. 'Favored one' referred to the Virgin's abundant virtues and the favor of the Holy Spirit that had come to rest on her. And there was one extraordinary dowry that had been stored up for her: the pledge of the immortal Bridegroom and the breaking of the first curse that our first mother's deception and disobedience called down on us. But now the gift of eternal joy and the new revelation of the bounteous unwed Bridegroom took the place of grief and distress. These two things were the stuff of the archangel's greeting. And then he continued: *The Lord be with you*! Meaning that all the riches of the King were hers; such was the fulfillment of the promise, the very Word of God, the Word too great for words, entered into the Virgin Mary's womb. The human nature was united with Him not by seed, but by the power of the Most High and the advent of the Holy Spirit. He Himself was both the Joiner and the Joined, who united both natures into a single substance, and who by grace was likewise fused with the human nature. He Himself built the temple of His flesh as he saw fit. That is what the words, 'the Lord be with you!' signify. It was He who broke the power of the ancient curse that had been cast on all women; that is why the man was chosen to be lord over the woman, and the woman had received the command: *and to your husband will you come back* (Gen. 3:16). For this reason and because of the first disobedience, childbirth had been plagued with grief and pain, as the prophet testifies; this is why the mother writhes in pain when the labors of childbirth come upon her. And so there is no end to the toil, hardship, and pain of women; but when the archangel spoke to the Virgin: 'Greetings, favored one', the whole debt of sorrow was put to flight. 'The Lord be with you!' and the dominion of man as well as the pain of childbirth are lifted from you; so she was a true Virgin among all virgins before, during, and after giving birth, the eternal and immaculate Virgin. And this grace of eternal virginity was not all He gave her, but by this she became chief of all virgins, and through her any woman who wished could be initiated into the choir of virgins. In fact, until then women did not have the ability to remain virgins, but the blessed, the most holy and eternal virgin Mary Mother of God was the leader and effective cause of women's virginity, those who wished; so indeed she became the source of all good things, and she, the magnificent and Most Holy Mother of our Lord and God and Savior Jesus Christ, became the helper of both men and women, the adornment and glory of the human nature, the joy of angels, helper of mankind, and strength of all who believe.

How perfect and all-encompassing is the end of the archangel's address in particular! *Blessed are you among women*, or, 'more than all women', for because of you women themselves were made worthy of the blessing, just as the men on account of your Son; but now both you and your Son have blessed the respective natures of men and women in general. And just as the curse, the pain, and the sorrow came from Adam, beginning with Eve both for men and women, in the same way the joy and blessing were poured out over all, beginning with you and your Son.

But let us consider how the holy Virgin reacted and responded with all understanding and wisdom. Of course, she did not resist nor disbelieve the promise, nor did she take it lightly. But like Isaiah when he was sent out as a prophet, she showed equal obedience (Is. 6:8), even if the unlikeliness of the thing caught her off guard. And unlike Zachariah's flat disbelief, she took the middle road; though she was startled, as was natural, she was not frightened at the sight of the archangel, since she had become used to his frequent visits when he brought her food in the temple; but she was disturbed by the words that echoed in her ears. This is why the divine messenger explained them to her and spoke accordingly. *When she saw him she was startled at his word and wondered what kind of greeting this was*, for doubtless she did not know the full scope of the mystery; and though she rejoiced at the union of divine and human natures, she wondered how it would come to pass. But Gabriel, the wondrous bringer of good news, without the Virgin even speaking a word about this, since he is a divine spirit and tester of spirits, he searched her mind and perceived her thought. And not only did he assuage her fear, but he also gave her a share of his joy and announced the ineffable birth: *Fear not, Mary, for you have found favor with God.* This favor that she had found was the honor and name of 'Theotokos'; that is why she was called, and is indeed, the Mother of God. And it is truly a great 'favor you have found with God' to become the Mother of the only-begotten Son of God. O grace surpassing all other graces, which can be apprehended with the soul but not expressed by the tongue!

And now let us pay close attention and consider the glory of the unwed bride and the dowry of her virginity. Let us explore the angel's brief and clear revelation: *And behold! you will conceive in your womb and bear a son and you will call his name Jesus!* When he told her, 'behold! you will conceive', at the moment he said it, he recognized the miraculous conception within her. "And you will bring a Son into the world and name him Jesus", he tells her. He has no earthly father, but is fatherless according to human descent, just as he is motherless according to His birth before the ages. Thus you will give birth to a child without the mediation of a father and will give him the name Jesus, which translated means 'Savior'; since you will never experience any of what usually happens to women, not even the pangs of childbirth, but just as you conceived without seed, so you will give birth immaculately and painlessly to the Savior of the whole world, and this fact will be made clear by the name. *He will be great and will be called Son of the Most High* on account of His human nature. He says this not of His divine nature, since in accordance with that He is above all glory, but about His human nature he says, 'He will be great and will be called Son of the Most High'. Not only because of His hypostatic union with the divine nature, but also because His miraculous deeds will give credence to His name; this is why he told her, 'you will call his name Jesus'. But also His Heavenly Father will later call him His beloved Son (Mt. 3:17; 17:5) and when

He begins to work countless wonders, He will be recognized by all reasonable people to be the Son of the Most High. *And the Lord God will give him the throne of David his father* (Lk. 1:32); this also he said as regards His human nature, since by it He began His proclamation and received those who believed in His name, those who recognized Him as heir to the throne of David and the house of Jacob. *And He will reign over the house of Jacob forever. And of His kingdom there will be no end*; he speaks of His never-ending kingdom not only concerning His divinity, but also His humanity, since there is no end to His dominion over both His natures. He will reign over those who accept Him, who have believed in Him as eternal King. So now He will reign over those who will believe in his word, and finally He will reign over all, as the sublime Paul says, "*but when he says that all things are subject* (1 Cor. 15:25-28), meaning when His kingdom is complete, *until He puts all enemies under His feet*, meaning, "when all things are subdued under His feet;" *but when all things are subjected to Him, then the Son Himself will be subject to Him who put all things under Him*, meaning to God the Father, since subjection is fitting for our nature that He bore; but because of this nature we have His achievements made our own.

But here you see the wisdom of the blessed and most holy Virgin and her extreme love of virginity. She accepted the archangel's message but was taken aback at his words. This is why she responded: *How will this happen to me, since I have not known a man?* "This," she says, "is impossible, since I am immaculate, consecrated to God; and clearly no one can conceive without a man." As the words of the godly Fathers have shown us long ago, this demonstrates how much she feared and worried that she might be stripped of her virginity that she had borne in the depths of her heart, and that is why she could not conceive of not remaining a virgin until the end. For she was fully unaware not only of the reality of marriage but even of desire, since she from the beginning she had been trained in perfect holiness and purity of soul and body. And she had never had the slightest thought or desire to compromise with any passion. Thus she outstripped the heights and depths of all human nature. This is why the King and Creator of all was pleased with the beauty of her soul, He who sees thoughts and *tests hearts and kidneys* (Ps. 7:10). He purified his dwelling place and saw fit to take up abode within her and be clothed by her with our nature. This is why her announcer, who had made known to her the ineffable mystery, delivered her from distress and explained to her the inexplicable birth, just as the blessed Apostle Luke says: A*nd the angel answered and said to her; the Holy Spirit will come upon you and the power of the Most High will overshadow you*"; you ask 'how will this happen to me since I have not known a man?'. There is no man needed here; your situation is different than that of all other women, just as that of your Son that you will bear must not be like the other people's children, who by disobedience conceive, carry and give birth 'in sin' (Ps. 50:7). Your conception will not be of such nature as to destroy your virginity, but rather will be all the more the seal and guardian of immaculacy and the herald of purity. Thus the Holy Spirit will come upon you first to adorn you as a bride worthy of the Lord, to make your soul, holy and adorned with so many virtues, most holy from the beginning, as well as your body. And at the same time, your immortal Bridegroom and Son, who is the power of the Most High, will overshadow you; for Christ is the power and the wisdom of God. He Himself will overshadow and make the surpassingly holy temple of His body in your immaculate womb. In this way, the immaterial and bodiless One will be clothed by you with a visible and material body, the power and *the brightness* (cf. Heb. 1:3) of the Father will overshadow your nature; the Word of God will take His flesh from you; the invisible God will be made visible as a man, and the Son of God will be made and called the 'Son of Man' on your account; your son will be called 'the Son of the Most High', and your virginity will remain hereafter untarnished and untouched.

O what wonderful and tremendous works! O what inexpressible and inscrutable mysteries! And yet, despite the apparent humbleness of your miraculous conception and supernatural birth, you received it faithfully as the greatest miracle and considered that He who is born of you will be called holy and the Son of the Most High; He will be able to do whatever He wills. *Now indeed, Elizabeth your relative has also conceived a son in her old age; and this is now the sixth month for her who was called barren. For with God nothing will be impossible* (Lk. 1:36-37). But in truth, all that He wills, He accomplishes at once; He searches outs the depth of the wisdom and the unshakeable holiness of the blessed Virgin. But in a moment of human hesitation (for according to the laws of nature such a conception was impossible) she said: *How can this be, since I do not know a man?* (Lk. 1:34). Although you are an archangel and proclaim to me miracles that surpass nature, nevertheless, it is impossible for me to be joined with a man, inasmuch as you are speaking to me of conception. But when the archangel explained to her that *the Holy Spirit will come upon her and the power of the Highest will overshadow her*, he filled her with joy and convinced her that nothing is impossible for God. She did not grow haughty, neither did she think lofty thoughts, but she put on humility and even greater contrition. And Mary said reverently: *Behold the maidservant of the Lord! Let it be to me according to your word* (Lk. 1:38). Then the angel left her, having completed the service he had been appointed, and he was astonished at the beauty of her virginity. Meanwhile, the holy Virgin had to keep this great secret hidden in her heart, for she was full of wisdom and the mother of wisdom. In fact, she did not even relate the angel's message to Joseph, nor to anyone else in those days. For this reason, certain Fathers interpret the word of the evangelist about Joseph, that he *did not know her till she had brought forth her firstborn Son* (Mt. 1:25), to mean that he did not know this secret, neither the angel's message nor the supernatural conception. If he had known these things, how would he have had any misgivings or considered her pregnancy a disgrace to himself? How could he have thought to *put her away secretly* (Mt. 1:19) until he had seen the angel in a vision? So these miracles were made manifest later, at the Lord's Birth: that is, the annunciation to the shepherds and the arrival of the wisemen, led by the star.

So thereupon the *highly favored* (cf. Lk. 1:28) Virgin recognized within herself the realization of the great event that had been foretold. But at the time of the archangel's annunciation, no one perceived the miracle.

The bride of God withdrew at once to her cousin Elizabeth, who just like her was rich in virtues, in order to confirm the truth of the angel's words concerning Elizabeth, who was also with child.

When she arrived at her cousin's house, and Elizabeth heard her greeting, at once *the voice* (cf. Mk. 1:3) of the Word, *the lamp* (cf. Jn. 5:35) of the light, *the prophet* of Grace (cf. Mt. 21:26), heard the sound of the greeting. And with a leap, he returned the greeting and worshipped the King who would be born and be baptized by himself; the One who would call him His prophet (cf. Lk. 7:26), His forerunner (cf. Lk. 7:27), and His baptizer (cf. Mk. 1:9). And so his mother also called out to the mother of the Lord: *Then she spoke out with a loud voice and said, "Blessed are you among women, and blessed is the fruit of your womb! But why is this granted to me, that the mother of my Lord should come to me? For indeed, as soon as the voice of your greeting sounded in my ears, the babe leaped in my womb for joy. Blessed is she who believed, for there will be a fulfillment of those things which were told her from the Lord"* (Lk. 1:42-45). Then she told the Mother of the Lord all that had happened to her, the shame of her barrenness, how her husband Zachariah was serving in his priestly ministry and burning incense when the archangel gave him his message, how he was struck dumb and not allowed to speak because of his doubt. (He had told these things to his wife Elizabeth in writing.) And so it became clear to the Virgin that Elizabeth's words to her truly did come from the Holy Spirit, just as the holy Gospel says: *[...] and Elizabeth was filled with the Holy Spirit. Then she spoke out with a loud voice and said, "Blessed are you among women, and blessed is the fruit of your womb!"* (Lk. 1:41-42), for she had been told by the Holy Spirit that Mary was with child and had conceived without a man. And this is why she called it 'the fruit of her womb', because the substance of the holy body was the product only of her womb and no other seed. The fruit of her womb is blessed because it is the true fruit that feeds the whole world, as David testifies: *All wait upon You to give them their food in due season. When You have given it them, they will gather it; and when You have opened your hand, they shall all be filled with good* (Ps. 103, 27-28; cf. Ps. 144, 15-16). And He Himself would go on to give us spiritual food as well, His precious and most holy body and blood (cf. Jn. 6:55).

The fruit of your womb is truly blessed, O spotless Virgin! He who broke the curse that lay upon us from the fruit of disobedience (cf. Gen. 3:6; 14-19). That fruit drove us out of Paradise, but this blessed fruit that came from your womb has opened unto us the door to paradise and has even led us to heaven and proclaimed us the heirs of Paradise.

Blessed are you among women, and blessed is the fruit of your womb! For the fruits of other women were born under the curse that came from the sin of the first Adam and Eve; and the curse came into the world through fleshly marriage and the corruption of sin. But only this other fruit, the fruit of your own womb, is blessed, for it ripened not by the seed of man nor within the corruption of sin, but was clothed by you in an unsown and incorruptible body; it committed no sin at all, and *there was no deceit found in His mouth* (Is. 53:9; 1 Pet. 2:22). And not only is He Himself blessed and without sin, but by His divine grace He has conferred this blessing also on the human nature with which He was joined, that was found under the curse, as the utterly blessed *Lamb of God, who took away the sins of the world* (Jn. 1:29). And so, this *blessed, highly favored* Mary, once she had been rendered a mother by supernatural means, while remaining a Virgin in soul and body, she then gained the power to prophesy about others. That is, she herself uttered truly prophetic words, full of grace, prayer, and foresight; that is to say, she was filled with the Holy Spirit, as the Gospel writer tells us. And Mary said: *My soul magnifies the Lord, and my spirit has rejoiced in God my Savior. For He has regarded the lowly state of His maidservant; For behold, henceforth all generations will call me blessed* (Lk. 1:46-48). Her heart was full of all humility, peace, and piety, and for this reason her God and Savior looked upon her as the prophet says: *[...] and upon whom will I look, but upon the humble and meek, and the one that trembles at My words?* (Is. 66:2). God found the blessed Mary to be such and looked upon her, for He saw that there was none like her in the race of men. For this reason He saw fit to dwell within her and gladly accepted a human body from her, with which He also went out to seek the lost (cf. Lk. 19:10). For the goal of His incarnation is the deification of man. And the Most High made Mary surpassingly holy and blessed by all generations.

With these words, the blessed mother of God confirmed what Elizabeth had said of her, as well as the words and the message of the archangel, which he had spoken in the name of the Lord; for Elizabeth had said: *Blessed is she who believed, for there will be a fulfillment of those things which were told her from the Lord* (Lk. 1:45). And the words of the archangel were likewise from the Lord, for He had sent him.

Thus she who had received grace also gave thanks to God and glorified His holy name, calling herself 'lowly' and a 'maidservant', and prophesying: [...] *henceforth all generations will call me blessed.* The angelic hosts truly do call her blessed, and the generations of men do likewise. Those who do not call her blessed and do not glorify her are not counted among mankind but are children of destruction and the portion of the Devil. For all true generations of mankind will call her blessed and glorify her and beseech her as their helper and mediator unto the Lord.

How full of grace and wisdom are the following words! *For He who is mighty has done great things for me, and holy is His name. And His mercy is on those who fear Him from generation to generation* (Lk. 1:49-50). His name and His mercy are 'the only-begotten Son' who out of compassion toward those who fear Him brought to pass the incarnation; He the holy Virgin as the first fruits, that he might show mercy to those who suffer and seek the lost sheep. But how can the Son also be called the 'Father' (cf. Is. 8:6)? Because the Father was made known through the Son, just as the Lord Himself said: *I have manifested Your name to men* (Jn. 17:6).

He has shown the strength of His arm (Lk. 1:51): that is, through His Son, who is called 'the arm of God' (cf. Ps. 43:4), as well as 'the power of God and the wisdom of God' (1 Cor. 1:24), 'the image of God' (2 Cor. 4:4), 'the express image of His person' (Heb. 1:3), and 'the right hand of the Most High' (Ps. 76:11). It is He, therefore, whom she called the 'arm' of God, for through Him God the Father *has scattered the proud in the imagination of their hearts. He has put down the mighty from their thrones* (Lk. 1:51-52). That is, "the rulers of the earth", the evil demons who have tyrannized the race of man from the moment of the first disobedience and the fall into sin, compelling us to commit sin and constant disobedience.

But when the Son by the will of the Father was clothed in flesh through the Holy Spirit and the Virgin Mary, He overthrew the boastfulness and the resistance of the haughty demons and *put down the mighty from their thrones*, locking them in *chains of darkness* to be delivered over to punishment, as the Apostle Peter says (cf. 2 Pet. 2:4). Thus He routed the invisible enemies, the renegade demons and wicked kings that persecute the faithful. He overthrew them, casting them down from their positions of power and frustrating their schemes. He has *exalted the lowly. He has filled the hungry with good things, and the rich He has sent away empty* (Lk. 1:52-53) and put to shame. And indeed, the poor fishermen, *uneducated and untrained* (Acts 4:13), those lowly and despised men He exalted in word and deed, appointing them the Apostles to the whole world, so that *their voice went out into all the earth, and their words to the ends of the world* (cf. Ps. 18:5). Thus they were revered by kings and rulers honored by the people (cf. Acts 4:16). To them He entrusted the Kingdom of Heaven (cf. Mt. 16:19) and made them blessed in the present world and in the world to come. Truly, He exalted the lowly and blessed Apostles by His infinite greatness. *He has filled the hungry*: the heathen peoples who were hungry for the word of God and deprived of the teaching and the knowledge of God, and this He gave by the preaching of the Apostles. He filled them with the godly teachings of the Holy Spirit and with knowledge of the divine mysteries. But the rich, those who had fallen away because of the vain musings of worldly wisdom and the proud He sent away in disgrace, for they were guilty by their own folly, as it is written: *I will destroy the wisdom of the wise and will bring to naught the understanding of the prudent* (Is. 29:14; cf. 1 Cor. 1:19).

He has helped His servant Israel in remembrance of His mercy, as He spoke to our fathers, to Abraham and to his seed forever (Lk. 1:54-55). He received as sons those Israelites who obeyed, those who believed in His word and were made worthy of divine adoption through His only-begotten Son, intellects who gaze upon God; for this is what the name "Israel" means: "an intellect that sees God". These are Abraham's true descendants (cf. Gal. 3:7; Lk. 3:8), and to them will He fulfill *the oath which He swore to our Father Abraham* (Lk. 1:73). The fulfillment is Christ, who took on flesh for us as the *Firstborn of all creation* (Col. 1:15); but by His grace, all who believed in His holy name have become children of God, as John the Evangelist says: *But as many as received Him, to them He gave the right to become children of God, to those who believe in His name* (Jn. 1:12). And the Apostle Paul says: *But it is not that the word of God has taken no effect. For they are not all Israel who are of Israel, nor are they all children because they are the seed of Abraham; but, "In Isaac your seed shall be called." That is, those who are the children of the flesh, these are not the children of God; but the children of the promise are counted as the seed* (Rom. 9:6-8): those who have believed in the word of the Lord and been baptized in the name of the Father and of the Son and of the Holy Spirit, be they Jews or gentiles, have become Christians and learned to carry out the Lord's commandments. These are called by the name of 'Israel' and 'servants of God', and to them is fulfilled the word of the mother of God: *He has helped His servant Israel in remembrance of His mercy*.

And Mary remained with her about three months and returned to her house (Lk. 1:56), for after the death of her blessed parents, the holy Virgin had had Elizabeth as a mother. This is why as soon as she had received Gabriel's annunciation she immediately *ran with haste* (Lk. 1:39) to greet Elizabeth and to tell her the words that had been proclaimed to her from the Lord. And out of divine love and daughterly devotion she *remained with her about three months*, as the holy Gospel says. When the time was coming for Elizabeth to give birth and the Virgin began to see the signs of her own pregnancy, she returned to the house of Joseph without telling him the archangel's message.

III: THE BIRTH

Now, when Joseph saw that she was with child, he was grieved; for he did not know the great secret, and, being *a just man* (Mt. 1:19), it pained him to see the Law of God flouted within his own home and cast doubt on himself as well. Moreover he was loath to humiliate Mary by handing her over to the chief priests to be punished. And yet, because he was adorned with every virtue and lived a holy life, he felt afflicted and wretched. This is why he *was minded to put her away secretly* from his house. *But while he thought about these things, behold, an angel of the Lord appeared to him in a dream, saying, "Joseph, son of David, do not be afraid* (Mt. 1:20) of this thing, nor of the sanctions of the Law; and do not harbor any doubts about Mary to whom you are betrothed by the law of men." He considered his betrothed as his future wife, but she had not been given to him in marriage as other women are – God forbid! But he was betrothed to her in order to protect the divine treasure devoted to the Lord. "Do not be afraid," the angel says to him, "to keep her in your home, *for that which is conceived in her is of the Holy Spirit. And she will bring forth a Son, and you shall call His name Jesus, for He will save His people from their sins"* (Mt. 1:20-21). With these words, the angel dispelled the fear that had plagued Joseph and in its place put on him another fear: that he must revere the holy Virgin as filled with the Holy Spirit and as the bearer of the unspeakable and inscrutable Word, according to the flesh; and yet He was begotten before all the ages, and would *save His people from their sins.* This is why the loving King came down from heaven to the earth to deliver us who believe in Him and worship Him from the slavery of sin and the power of the evil demons.

And so the prophecy of Jacob the Patriarch was fulfilled, which says: *A ruler shall not fail from Judah, nor a prince from his loins, until there come the things stored up for him; and he is the expectation of nations* (Gen. 49:10). He, Christ the Lord, is truly the expectation of nations and of those Israelites who believed in His holy name. For *they are not all children because they are the seed of Abraham; but, "In Isaac your seed shall be called"* (Rom. 9:7). Not all those who are born of Israel are called by the name of 'Israel', but those who have received the proclamation of the Gospel, as we have mentioned. Simeon tells us this same thing, for he calls Him *a light to bring revelation to the Gentiles and the glory of Your people Israel*

(Lk. 2:32): that is, to those who believe. And he calls them all by one name, for He came for the salvation of all His people. *For my eyes have seen Your salvation, which You have prepared before the face of all peoples* (Lk. 2:30). So how can he say, *A ruler shall not fail from Judah*? And why did the Lord Himself come instead? Because He Himself was the Lord of all and the true King, and because He arose from the tribe of Judah (cf. 2 Kgd. 7:16)! So it is clear that the Patriarch's prophecy did not refer to some spiritual king but was speaking of the flesh-and-blood kings of the world. This is why the Lord said: *My Kingdom is not of this world* (Jn. 18:36), for at the time when He said that, the kings of Judah's line had failed and the Roman Emperors ruled all of Judea. So the Savior was King of both the Romans and all the nations who believed in His holy name. I am not merely speaking of the Kingdom He possesses by right of His nature and divinity – for He is *King and Lord for ever and ever and ever* (Ex. 15:18) - but also of the willing submission of all the faithful to Him. For He called all those who submit to His Kingship by a new and matchless name: "True Christian". This is the precious name that He has bestowed on us.

So when all the might and dominion of the Jews had failed, and all the world had submitted to the rule of Rome, *in those days*, says the holy Gospel, *a decree went out from Caesar Augustus that all the world should be registered* (Lk. 2:1). That was when the true King and Savior of all the world was born. This was designed by His providence, that the rulers from the tribe of Judah should utterly cease just as all the imperial power passed into the hands of the Romans. The Hebrews were ruled *with an iron scepter* (cf. Ps. 2:9), which is the might of Rome; they were called 'an iron scepter' because they truly did *crush* the Jews following the passion and resurrection of Christ, exiling them forever. It was thus the work of Christ's providence that the Romans should rule over the Jews, but that He in turn should rule over the Romans and all other nations, including those Jews who believed; and He is King unto the ages over all creation.

But these visible events are a manifestation of invisible mysteries. The census that took place here is a pattern of another census, for the dominion of Caesar over all things announced the unrivaled dominion of the only true God and King of all things. So this census prefigured the willing submission of all and the heavenly census of every man who so wishes. And just as the *decree went out* into all the earth, so also the proclamation of Christ has gone out into all the earth (cf. Rom. 10:18). And when it says He went up *to his own city* (Lk. 2:3), it is teaching us that we all need to return to our first homeland and city, from where we have been driven out and scattered amongst various lands and walks of life. The taxes paid to Caesar (cf. Mk. 12:13-17) represent the spiritual fruits of charity, a good life and holy prayer that we must offer to God. And by Heaven's providence, this decree obligated Joseph to go to his hometown in Judea, from Nazareth to Bethlehem, and in this way, he fulfilled two prophecies. The first had foretold that *He shall be called a Nazarene* (Mt. 2:23), and the second, that the Messiah would come from Bethlehem (cf. Mic. 5:2; 1 Kgd. 16:1). For the annunciation and the divine conception took place in Nazareth, and the wonderful birth occurred in Bethlehem. So do you see the twofold humility of the rich King who became poor for us? For the town of Nazareth was held in contempt because no prophet had ever come from there, as Nathanael says: *Can anything good come out of Nazareth?* (Jn. 1:47). And Bethlehem, although she had been honored to bring forth David the Prophet, was otherwise utterly impoverished and lowly, and this is why the Prophet consoles her saying: *'But you, Bethlehem, in the land of Judah, are not the least among the rulers of Judah; for out of you shall come a Ruler, who will shepherd My people Israel'* (Mt. 2:6). Josef was a citizen of Bethlehem, and as often happens, Joseph left his hometown to move to another city and wanted to build a house in Nazareth. Now, while he was living there, because of his righteousness and piety, Joseph took the Virgin Mary from the priests to be his betrothed, and it was there that the archangel announced to him the great and puzzling message.

So when the decree went out from Caesar Augustus that the entire empire should be registered, and each man went to be registered in his hometown, *Joseph also went up from Galilee, out of the city of Nazareth, into Judea, to the city of David, which is called Bethlehem, because he was of the house and lineage of David, to be registered with Mary, his betrothed wife, who was with child* (Lk. 2:4-5) by the Holy Spirit. The time was coming for her to give birth, but the Emperor's decree required Mary to go up to Bethlehem as well, for she also was *of the house and lineage of David*; and in this way, divine providence guided them to Bethlehem.

Meanwhile, the message that Joseph had received from the angel required him to minister to Mary with reverence. This is why his other sons and relatives had already been sent off to be registered beforehand, but he himself came much later with Mary and his daughters; and when they reached Jerusalem and Bethlehem, the time came for the wondrous and miraculous birth. But because such a multitude had gathered for the census, and all the lodgings were already taken, including the houses in Bethlehem as well, they decided to stay in a cave in Bethlehem. O what utter humiliation and exile you underwent for our sake, Lord of all! There was no place nor inn found for Him. And so the Uncontainable and Uncircumscribable was held within a small cave and an unseemly manger. The Word of God, the uncreated and unapproachable One, the Maker of all the world, led His mother to the cave in Bethlehem, as the holy Gospel says: *And so it was, that while they were there, the days were completed for her to give birth. And she brought forth her firstborn Son, and wrapped Him in swaddling cloths, and laid Him in a manger, because there was no room for them in the inn* (cf. Lk. 2:6-7). So the Lord of heaven and earth was wrapped *in swaddling cloths.* O wonder of wonders! He who gives food to all things nursed milk Himself, and the great Census-Taker took part in the census Himself (cf. Ps. 86:5-6). And thus was fulfilled the prophecy of David concerning Bethlehem and the birth of the Lord, saying: *I will not give sleep to my eyes, nor slumber to my eyelids, nor rest to my temples, until I find a place for the Lord, a tabernacle for the God of Jacob. Behold, we heard of it in Ephratha; we found it in the fields of the wood* (Ps. 131:4-6). This he said of Bethlehem, where the Lord was born. So he continues: *Let us enter into His tabernacles: let us worship at the place where His feet stood* (Ps. 131:7). Who then can speak of the immeasurable humility of the Lord of hosts and *cause all His praises to be heard?* (Ps. 105:2).

Meanwhile, Elizabeth, the venerable mother of the Forerunner, was present for most of the Lord's birth, for she had not yet fled to the hills to save herself and her son. But since she was a prophetess and a witness of the holy Virgin's conception, so likewise she was the glorious guardian of her house and eyewitness of the events; and thereafter she would bear testimony and zealously proclaim the divine manner in which the Virgin had given birth. She was filled with joy and gladness at the sublime birth as at a marvelous feast.

So then, *the middle wall of separation* (Eph. 2:14) had fallen, and the bitter enmity was resolved; peace and love had been poured out on all creation: God had become man, and heaven and earth were now one (cf. Rev. 21:3). The angels had deigned to show themselves to the shepherds, and the shepherds shone with the angels' light, overjoyed at the great tidings. Away they sped in their gladness to see *the good Shepherd* (cf. Jn. 10:11), like a spotless, newborn lamb within the cave. The earth gave ear to the heavens' anthem and the heavenlies were filled with joy at the *peace on earth, goodwill toward men* (Lk. 2:14).

All the while, though the shepherds were trembling with fear at the wonders they had seen, an angel of light dispelled their fear and announced joy to them: *Fear not! for behold, I bring you good tidings of great joy which will be to all people. For there is born to you this day in the city of David a Savior, who is Christ the Lord. And this will be the sign to you: You will find a Babe wrapped in swaddling cloths, lying in a manger." And suddenly there was with the angel a multitude of the heavenly host praising God and saying: "Glory to God in the highest, and on earth peace, goodwill toward men!"* (Lk. 2:10-14). Once they had seen and heard these fearsome things, the terrified shepherds set off into the night to find the Savior in Bethlehem, the light of the whole world (cf. Jn. 1:9).

But Mary kept all these words and pondered them in her heart (Lk. 2:19). Not only the words of the shepherds, but all that she had heard from back when she was living in the Temple, and after she had left there and heard the angel's Annunciation and the immaculate conception, the painless birth and her virginity that was untouched by it. She also pondered how she alone of all women had been spared the pangs of childbirth and become a mother while remaining a Virgin; but even she could not comprehend how she had given birth. Observe how these events were ordained by God and the two natures were united: the miraculous Son did not reveal to His mother the secret of His own Birth, and in a flash, without her even realizing how, he appeared outside of her womb, resting on the throne of her hands (cf. Ps. 21:10-11). And so the birth was free of corruption and beyond comprehension, just as the conception was immaculate and unfathomable.

The dew on Gideon's fleece was an ancient pattern of this glorious and miraculous Birth (cf. Jdg. 6:37-40). But the reality transcended the pattern; in fact, though the dew condensed slowly and of its own accord on the fleece, it could not be wrung out by hand. But this divine dew that gives life to all things entered into the Virgin's womb without commotion or passion; and likewise it left the immaculate mother's womb without her knowledge or perception, inexplicably; but being clothed by her in human flesh, it departed as easily and sublimely as it had entered. He Himself did not make the manner of His birth known, neither to others nor to His own mother. These were the inexpressible and inscrutable marvels that the most Holy Mary *kept and pondered in her heart*. And she was overjoyed at all these things, and considered how God Himself had been born of her, He who had glorified His incorruptible mother and made her worthy to be venerated by all generations, supremely blessed and highly praised in heaven and on earth.

So then, when the shepherds heard the gladsome tidings that the Lord of glory had been born, they set out for Bethlehem, proclaiming to all men what they had seen and heard concerning the glorious child, *and all those who heard it marveled at those things which were told them by the shepherds* (Lk. 2:18). And immediately thereafter behold! the wisemen came *from the East*, led by the star that had told them that the newborn babe was the Lord of heaven and earth. Now, this star was no fixture of the material firmament, but a noetic power sent from on high that confounded their astrological calculations and dispelled the darkness by its erratic course; for its track was not like that of the other stars, but it progressed haltingly, and kept the pace and direction of those it was leading. Sometimes it would move, other times it would stand still; sometimes it would appear, and other times it would vanish from their sight. Moreover it described a course from North to South, for that was the direction from Persia to Judaea. And it did not appear high up in the sky but moved close to the earth until it reached that tiny village. It even entered into that humble cave and, most wondrous of all, it shone not only by night, but also by day. Its light was so bright that it outshone and eclipsed the sun, and this not just one or two days, but until it had led the wisemen from Persia to Jerusalem and Bethlehem. And yet, it did not appear to them at the birth of Christ, but much earlier, in order to silence those who would seek to calculate the time of His birth. It appeared to them long in advance and informed their hearts of the birth of the King; it likewise urged them to return by a different, roundabout way. And so it clearly demarcated the time of their arrival and how long they remained, so that they found the *King of glory* (cf. Ps. 23:7) resting in the manger. None of these things are in keeping with the nature and behavior of a common star, but this light was clearly a rational power who knew all that had transpired and led them accordingly, following the command of the Creator and Ordainer of all things (cf. Num. 24:17).

And it was not in vain that it led them to Jerusalem, though they lost sight of it as soon as they arrived. This happened for two reasons: First, by appearing to all the inhabitants of Jerusalem, it wanted to tell them of this mystery, above all through the searching and questioning of the wisemen: *Where is He who has been born King of the Jews? For we have seen His star in the East and have come to worship Him* (Mt. 2:2). At these words, the whole city was thrown into an uproar, and Herod was terrified. And second, so that even the Lord's enemies, the scribes and the Pharisees, could testify and reveal the time and the place of His birth, even bringing forth the Prophet as a witness, saying: *But you, Bethlehem, in the land of Judah, are not the least among the rulers of Judah; For out of you shall come a Ruler who will shepherd My people Israel* (Mt. 2:6; cf. Mic. 5:2). For indeed, the other rulers were known for their carnal pleasures, but they were not shepherds, for they did not give their lives for the sheep. But He is the true Shepherd, for he leads the flock that follows Him in the way of life, to the *green pastures* (cf. Ps. 22:2) of Paradise, and *lays down His life for His sheep* (Jn. 10:11). Therefore, consider how the words of the Patriarch Jacob and Micah the Prophet converge: For Jacob spoke of the coming of the Lord out of Bethlehem, while Micah further specified that *the expectation of the nations* would appear at the end, when the rulers *of Judah* had failed (Gen. 49:10; Mic. 5:3). When the wisemen heard these prophecies and confirmed them with the appearance of the star, they proclaimed that the Christ is the true, long-awaited King.

When Herod learned this, he was disturbed, for he loved his power with a passion and feared lest his kingdom and rule be overthrown, for he was full of folly. So *when he had gathered all the chief priests and scribes of the people together, he inquired of them where the Christ was to be born* (Mt. 2:4). But they were wicked and only answered him in part, concealing the rest. They informed him that the Christ would be born in Bethlehem, as the Prophet says: *But you, Bethlehem, in the land of Judah, are not the least among the rulers of Judah; for out of you shall come a Ruler who will shepherd My people Israel* (Mt. 2:6; cf. Mic. 5:2). They failed to tell him, however, the Prophet's next words: *And his goings forth were from the beginning of days, even from eternity* (Mic. 5:2). For already by then they were jealous of the Christ and refused to recognize Him as

God. This is why they did not report the words that proclaim His glory; for they willfully closed their eyes and ears, lest they see and hear the truth, as Isaiah foretold (cf. Is. 6:9-10; Mt. 13:14-15). Nevertheless, Herod, seething with jealousy, called the wisemen to himself in secret and questioned them about the newborn King; he uttered wicked lies, claiming that he too wanted to go and worship Him, so when they found Him, they must tell him where the King of Kings is (cf. Mt. 2:7-8). This is the way people told each other about the birth of the King of the Jews. Herod was forced to rely on the wisemen and the Jews for information about the star's appearance. The wisemen, for their part, were fully convinced when they heard the Prophet's message and especially when they saw Herod's jealousy and fear. So when they left Jerusalem, their guiding star reappeared to them, closer and more radiant than the light of day. It shone brighter than the sun, leading them to the *Sun of righteousness* (cf. Mal. 4:2), the Maker of the sun, moon, stars, and all of creation. It led them into Bethlehem, as if it were leading them into heaven, into the poor cave and up to the beggarly manger.

So when it arrived at the place, it shone down on the object of their desire with even greater brilliance like a finger; and when it had completed its mission, it vanished from their sight.

Meanwhile, when they saw the star guiding them, or rather the angel manifesting itself in this form, *they rejoiced with exceedingly great joy*, for they had reached their goal. But then the great wonder happened, for truly, as they stood beside the newborn, the firstborn before the ages, they were filled at once with grace, happiness and light; an inexpressible joy was poured out in their hearts. And besides that, the vision and fellowship of the babe's unwed and uncorrupted mother were beyond all grace and glory, and the bloom of her physical health transcended all human experience. The birth had left on her no trace of pain or frailty, but on the contrary, after giving birth she was yet more radiant and lovely, for she was also filled with grace and the light of the divine birth; and this was a stunning miracle to all who saw it. The wisemen were filled to the brim with all these miracles and wonders, and they glorified the Lord in their joy *and fell down and worshipped Him* as King and God, *and when they had opened their treasures, they presented gifts to Him: gold, frankincense, and myrrh*, as to their King and God; to Him who took on flesh on our behalf and would go to His death that we might win immortality through Him. And the grace of the Holy Spirit had even instructed the wisemen to bring these gifts, as a pattern for us of the spiritual gifts we should bring. We must offer our good and holy life as 'gold', wisdom and spiritual contemplation as 'frankincense', and the mortification of the passions and the members of the body as 'myrrh'; through these we will attain dispassion and the Kingdom of Heaven.

And thus were fulfilled the words of the most blessed Virgin, which she had spoken before: *He who is mighty has done great things for me, and holy is His name*, and, *behold, henceforth all generations will call me blessed.* And indeed from that time onward, her majesties and her glory and devotion in all things began to manifest themselves, and steadily grew with time.

So this is how the wisemen found the One they sought. They saw before them the King of glory and worshipped Him. They offered visible gifts, and with them they also offered up themselves to the Lord as the foundation and forerunners of the nations that would return to Him and be accepted into the service of Christ. These wisemen were the first to believe in and worship Christ, His heralds and the witnesses of His Kingdom by their gifts and costly offerings; for they scorned the folly of the Jews and the heedless despotism of Herod. For since they had been told in a dream *that they should not return to Herod, they departed for their own country another way* (Mt. 2:12).

Therefore, just as Christ, the King of riches, chose to come into the world in poverty, and by so choosing made poverty honorable, so also, O believer, when you hear of this humility and poverty, and if you someday find yourself in poverty, do not be drawn away, but turn your mind away from the squalid cave and the unseemly abode and unto the highest heavens; away from the beggarly manger and unto the shining star and the chorus of angelic praise; away from the mean swaddling cloths and the tax collectors and unto the gifts and the veneration of the wisemen and the acceptance of the nations. Do not belittle the humility of the Lord, not even with your exalted theology, but rather set your hopes on the high and glorious blessings.

When His blessed mother saw all these things, her heart was filled all the more with faith, hope and love for her Son and King, and she so looked forward to the greater and more glorious things as if she could already see them happening. And all this overflowed when the other signs of His humility appeared: After the Lord had been born in the squalid cave and laid to rest in the beggarly manger, *and when eight days were completed for the circumcision of the Child, His name was called Jesus, the name given by the angel before He was conceived in the womb* (Lk. 2:21). This name gave voice to the extreme blessedness of exchanging the passion of His flesh for the gift of dispassion. After this, on the fortieth day, *they brought Him to Jerusalem to present Him to the Lord (as it is written in the Law of the Lord)* (Lk. 2:22-23).

Now, it might be expedient at this point to comment on where the accounts of the holy Gospel writers diverge; for Matthew speaks of the flight to Egypt, the rage of Herod, and the slaughter of the newborns as directly following the birth, while Luke mentions the fortieth day, the journey to Jerusalem, and Jesus' presentation at the temple as directly following the birth. Know then, that Matthew avoided mentioning the circumcision, the journey to Jerusalem, the presentation at the Temple, Simeon the God-receiver and the other events that took place in those days. What he did write, however, occurred much later, after two years or perhaps somewhat less (cf. Mt. 2:16): how Joseph saw the angel, fled to Egypt, and later returned out of Egypt. This is the actual sequence of events that Scripture gives: immediately after the preceding events, Matthew the Evangelist mentions things that took place much later. For instance, while he says that Joseph, *being warned by God in a dream, turned aside into the region of Galilee. And he came and dwelt in a city called Nazareth, that it might be fulfilled which was spoken by the prophets, "He shall be called a Nazarene"* (Mt. 2:22-23), he adds immediately after it: *In those days John the Baptist came preaching in the wilderness of Judea* (Mt. 3:1). So although John the Baptist did not come preaching for another thirty years, he connects this story with the nativity. He did the same thing when describing the Lord's birth, the arrival of the wisemen, their veneration, and their return home. Immediately afterwards, he added the flight of Joseph to Egypt together with the Lord and the holy Virgin Mother of God. Likewise, he spoke of the slaughter of the newborns and the other things just as the Holy Spirit had inspired him to write. While Luke wrote, by the grace of the same Holy Spirit, the events that directly followed the birth, which Matthew had left out (that is, how Jesus was circumcised, went up to Jerusalem and was presented at the temple, how the divine Baby was laid in Simeon's arms, and so on). This is because the task of describing the plan of salvation was not given to just one Gospel writer, but rather the first recorded certain events and miracles of the

Lord, and the second or the third or the fourth recorded others. This is our comment on how the Gospel writers complement each other.

But we must consider how Herod was both scorned and deceived by the wisemen, how his rage and madness were not made manifest from the beginning, but only after so much time had elapsed, and how he became so wicked and violent. And whether, as Luke did not mention, the child was hidden during this time or whether the wisemen themselves took care to hide the child and His mother (for they knew of Herod's rage), or urged them both to move to another place, as often happens. But indeed, we do have a description of this man's character. We have learned that in those days, when the wisemen came to Jerusalem and inquired about the birth of the child, and Herod in his jealousy lied and tried to find a way to murder Him under the pretense of wanting to worship Him, there was great commotion and disturbance, even in the very house of the king (cf. Mt. 2:3). But this was a dispensation of the divine plan of salvation, to give impetus to the search for the royal scion and the Lord of all creation. The contention and confusion reached even unto the members of Herod's own household. Ultimately, he himself was consumed and wreaked havoc all around him. He began by murdering his wife. He could not, however, murder his sons without an imperial decree. This drove him into a frenzy of mad rage against them. He made every effort to go to Rome and meet with the Emperor, so that he would grant him the power to murder them. And that is just what happened. On receiving permission, he promptly strangled his sons and glutted his raving, diabolical, depraved soul on their blood. And when the savagery of his heart had been spent on them, his aggression swelled to a climax and broke loose against everyone. When he considered the wisemen's search for the newborn King, the thought plunged him into the wildest delusions and paranoia. He was haunted by the fear that the child would take away his power, for he was a slave of the passion of luxury and power. He was filled with envy and rage, and though the wisemen were searching for only a single child, the King of all, he directed his wrath against all the innocent babes and slew by the sword *all the male children who were in Bethlehem and in all its districts, from two years old and under, according to the time which he had determined from the wisemen* (Mt. 2:16).

O cruel mind that *fights against God* (cf. Acts 5:39)! How could he shamelessly slaughter so many innocent creatures, when the heart of a man cannot even bear to slay even that many small animals, or even tear up that many fresh shoots of soulless plants? Much less execute so many infants blessed with reason! But the godless man has no qualms even about killing his own small children. O how twisted is the love of power and the envy it brings forth! It is the beginning of all evils. One of the archangels, by the honor that he had received from God, fell so far as to become a demon hostile to God, His sworn enemy, all on account of his thirst for power. He is the envy that made Belial himself (cf. 2 Cor. 6:15) and by him the whole Jewish nation into God-slayers; he made these wretches forget their Lord's countless good gifts (cf. Ps. 102:2). And in the same way, these two passions utterly dominated the godless Herod and made him into a murderer of children, first of his own and then of those innumerable innocent babes, and what is even worse, to contrive the execution of the very King and Lord of the Universe.

However, O Herod, enemy of God and devil's ally, if the words of the wisemen really were empty and false, why were you afraid and distraught? But if, on the other hand, they are true, and He who was heralded by the Prophets has come to the earth, how could you presume to think that you could murder Him? O you blind fool, your fierce envy has brought the wrath of God down upon your head, and you have lost your office and your life, and are become food for worms while you are still alive, as you well deserve. Even in this world your punishment was fearsome and awful to those who saw the wrath descend upon you; and on account of the everlasting One, you are given over into everlasting torment, the harshest and most dreadful, in the fires of Gehenna (cf. Mt. 5:22-30), in accordance with what you have done. But let us return and continue our discourse.

Once the vile Herod's savage decree had been issued, the whole multitude of innocent babes was brutally and mercilessly slain by the sword; like a wildfire it burned and razed not only Bethlehem and her surrounding villages to the ground, but also ravaged and laid waste to all of Judea. The Prophet had foreseen all of this long ago and had given voice to his sadness: *"A voice was heard in Ramah, lamentation, weeping, and great mourning, Rachel weeping for her children, refusing to be comforted, because they are no more* (Mt. 2:18; cf. Jer. 38:15). So now, when one sees these things laid out, this prophecy makes sense. Rachel was the mother of Benjamin, and when she died, she was buried in the same place, on the road to Ephratha, that is, Bethlehem (cf. Gen. 35:16-19; 1 Kgd. 10:2). Now, Ramah is a region belonging to the tribe of Benjamin. Benjamin was the son of

Rachel, and Rachel's grave lies near enough to the borders of Ramah (cf. Gen. 48:7) that great weeping can be heard from there. So it was because of Benjamin and the grave of his mother that these unjustly slain children were called 'the children of Rachel'. *Refusing to be comforted, because they are no more.*

This was no small catastrophe. There was no chance to flee or move away. The destruction and slaughter of the children of Rachel and Benjamin were complete; but this is precisely the reason why Bethlehem was chosen and so highly praised, not so much for any other virtues, but because of this very event: It fulfilled the Passover required of it by the law, and endured the sacrifice, not of some sheep devoid of reason, but many spotless lambs, gifted with reason. As soon as they were free of their mothers' wombs, they were transported by the sword out of the misery of this fleeting world and into eternity; no sooner had they seen the physical light of day, than they were robbed of it for the sake of the noetic light, this transient light in exchange for that everlasting light. These brave souls were spirited away into the unbroken light, those martyrs made perfect before their time, the fellow-children of Christ, without ever knowing the truth. They were slain for Christ and in His stead, the first of all the other martyrs. They were sacrificed on His account and for His sake, even before the passion He Himself endured on our behalf. For Christ's presence among men must rest on the foundation of a great sacrifice on their part.

This is why not only the virginity radiated by His most pure mother transcended thought and nature, but likewise also the virtue of the children slain for Christ and their nobility under trial; even the land was cleansed of the blood sacrificed to idols, all because of the shed blood of these innocent and holy children (cf. Dt. 32:43; Gen. 4:10); they were proven to be forerunners and harbingers of the glorious and divine blood of the King that would be shed and sprinkled on the Cross (Lev. 4-5:13; Heb. 12:24).

But we have said enough on this topic. Let us recall to mind the presentation of dearest Jesus at the temple and the events which followed; for all of these things are the praise and glory of His immaculate and supremely blessed mother. In fact, even when we speak of the Lord, our discourse concerns her as well, for there was perfect fellowship between them. Thus, all that pertains to Jesus naturally also relates to the theme of our discussion.

So then, on the eighth day after His birth, the child was circumcised and given the name "Jesus", as the archangel had instructed before the conception (Lk. 2:21). But this day was not only the eighth, but also the first, the Lord's Day. On this day, Sunday, the archangel delivered his message to the Virgin. On this day also the child was born of the Virgin. On this day He rose from the dead (cf. Lk. 24:1) and *resurrected together with Himself* (cf. Eph. 2:5-6) our mortal nature, bound under the curse. On this day, Sunday, we will all be raised together with Him, and He will come again in celestial glory to *judge the living and the dead* (cf. 2 Tim. 4:1; 1 Pet. 4:5). For these reasons this day is honored and hallowed among all the days of the week: the holy Sunday. For it is bound up with such great mysteries.

IV: PRESENTATION AT THE TEMPLE

Sometime later, on the fortieth day after Jesus' birth, *they brought Him to Jerusalem to present Him to the Lord (as it is written in the law of the Lord, "Every male who opens the womb shall be called holy unto the Lord")* (Lk. 2:22-23). We all know now that He is both the One who makes holy and the One who is holy (cf. Heb. 2:11). But we do not all know what was written and applied to every firstborn male that was presented before the Lord, according to the stipulation of the Law: They offered a sacrifice for it of *a pair of turtledoves or two young pigeons* (Lk. 2:24; Lev. 5:7). The 'turtledoves' teach us sobriety and love of solitude, and the 'two pigeons' teach us meekness and innocence. And while this precept of the Law was fulfilled by all, not all understood it in reality. Just as the other words and deeds of the Prophets were enigmatic and unintelligible to most people, so also this practice.

Not every firstborn male is, in fact, 'holy unto the Lord' (cf. Ex. 13:2). Many firstborns bear witness to this, like Cain, Ruben, Esau, and their successors. And moreover, not 'every male' *opens the womb*, for a woman's womb is 'opened' when she has intercourse with her husband and her virginity is lost; only afterwards does the son enter the world out of her womb, which has already been 'opened' prior to giving birth. And what is more, if every firstborn is holy at birth, then where does that leave this verse: *Behold, I was conceived in iniquities, and in sins my mother desired me* (Ps. 50:7)? For not only birth, but even conception follows the order and pattern of sin; and so the precept of the Law came to restore to Paradise the results of the Fall. And so now that the providence of the Creator desired to recreate us, He was pleased to make a different way for Him to be born who would increase our race (cf. Gen. 1:28; Jn. 1:13), a way without concupiscence and pain; but naturally not every firstborn male is 'called holy unto the Lord'.

But there is one and only one firstborn male who is 'holy unto the Lord': He whose conception was not the result of desire, of the seed of man (God forbid this blasphemy!), but by grace and the advent of the Holy Spirit; his birth was not simply a further continuation of the corruption and pangs of childbirth, but was accomplished by the power and wisdom of God Most High. And so the holy scion was born holy, and the holiest of holies, as Isaiah says (cf. Is. 6:3). And notwithstanding that the holy womb had to be opened at His birth, it nevertheless still remained closed, as Ezekiel says, the Seer of the unseen: *This gate shall be shut, it shall not be opened, and no one shall pass through it; for the Lord God of Israel shall enter by it, and it shall be shut* (Ez. 44:2). So truly, therefore, it remained shut through both conditions and sealed before the conception, at the conception, and after the conception and the birth. But how could it remain closed and at the same time be open, as the Prophet says: *Every male who opens the womb shall be called holy unto the Lord*? By nature of Mary's virginity, her womb remained closed and not open, but because of the almighty power of the begotten One, every closed door of nature opens and submits before Him. For whom else could open for himself the womb of his mother, and yet at the same time keep it closed, except for Him whose conception and birth are inexpressible, supernatural, and unfathomable? So you see the truth of the Prophecy: for he did not only say that the firstborn *would be called holy*, but *holy unto the Lord*. Who else could claim to be 'holy unto the Lord' even before his birth, if not He who had been heralded by the angel of the Lord: *Therefore, also, that Holy One who is born will be called the Son of God* (Lk. 1:35)? But as for the prophecy that *every male that opens the womb shall be called holy unto the Lord*, this was intended to hide the power of the Word within a general statement, for this mystery is truly the most hidden of all mysteries.

So let us listen attentively to the words of Simeon which he announced concerning Jesus, the dearest and most sought-after One. For indeed, what could be dearer and more valuable than poring over these words and all that concerns His holy and immaculate mother? What prophecies and blessings did this elder proclaim, this righteous, holy, and aged man? He had already reached the boundaries of this fleeting human life, and he was *waiting for the Consolation of Israel, and the Holy Spirit was upon him. And it had been revealed to him by the Holy Spirit that he would not see death before he had seen the Lord's Christ. So he came by the Spirit into the temple* (Lk. 2:25-27). That is, he was empowered by the Holy Spirit to take the long-awaited One into his arms and take his honored leave from the Newborn, out of this ephemeral life of sorrows and toil. Although the elder was frail and hunched with old age, at that moment he straightened up his wizened body and bounded over to the child, took the Lord into his arms and departed this brief and troubled life; this is a pattern of our aged and decrepit nature, which the Savior and Deliverer took upon Himself, in condescension and mercy coming to seek the lost and deliver us from the age-old bondage to the passions and out of the power of the demons and their many delusions, making it worthy of the grace of the Holy Spirit.

So what does the Gospel writer say of the just elder? *And behold, there was a man in Jerusalem whose name was Simeon, and this man was just and devout, waiting for the Consolation of Israel, and the Holy Spirit was upon him.* [...] *So he came by the Spirit into the temple. And when the parents brought in the Child Jesus, to do for Him according to the custom of the Law, he took Him up in his arms and blessed God and said: "Lord, now You are letting Your servant depart in peace, according to Your word; For my eyes have seen Your salvation, which You have prepared before the face of all peoples; a light to bring revelation to the Gentiles and the glory of Your people Israel"* (Lk. 2:25, 27-32). He was truly filled with the grace of the Holy Spirit, for his heart had been illuminated by the grace of Him whom he held in his hands. He began by offering thanks, for he recognized the fountain of goodness, and then went on to prophesy of his own departure out of this world, for his eyes had indeed seen Christ the Savior, whom until now he had only seen by noetic vision, the One whose name had been determined before the ages (cf. Is.9:6); but it remained hidden as a great mystery, and has now been revealed *before the face of all peoples* (cf. Eph. 1:9-10). Not only for the Jews, but for *all peoples; a light to bring revelation to the Gentiles and the glory of Your people Israel.* It was He who made the light to shine on *the people walking in darkness* (Is. 9:2; Mt. 4:16). He Himself was *the Light* (Jn. 1:9), the God and King and Maker of all, and the glory of His people Israel; that is, for *as many as received Him, to them He gave the right* to be called by the name of "Israel" (Jn. 1:12). Christ came down from heaven to earth by His mercy, in order to become the light and glory of them all; He was clothed in flesh by the Holy Spirit and the Virgin Mary. All this the Holy Spirit had revealed to the blessed elder: *And Joseph and His mother marveled at those things which were spoken of Him* (Lk. 2:33).

But you, O friend of God, see how the Gospel writer separated Joseph from the Virgin after she had given birth and his doubts had been resolved and allayed. For the birth was divine, and He who was born was of surpassing glory. This is why it says, *Joseph and His mother marveled at those things which were spoken of Him.* Joseph, he calls by name, for he was not the father of the child, nor was he His mother's husband. This is why he is simply called "Joseph". The blessed Virgin, however, is called 'his mother', and Simeon was well aware of this fact, for the Holy Spirit had granted him insight into these mysteries. He blessed both of them, for he knew that Joseph was a just man and a faithful minister to the mystery of the Lord. *Then Simeon blessed them, and said to Mary His mother* [...] (Lk. 2:34). He addresses himself specifically to the glorious Mary, for he knew that she was the treasure chamber of good and the receptacle of the greatest wonders, the helper of God in the marvelous Birth of His Son: *Behold, this Child is destined for the fall and rising of many in Israel* (Lk. 2:34).

Now consider the truth of these words: The salvation truly was prepared in a way that all peoples could see, for God's will is that all men be saved and deified (cf. 2 Pet. 3:9; 1 Tim. 2:4). But the 'fall' and the 'rising' depend on the people's own will; some of them believed and others did not believe, starting with Israel (cf. Rom. 11:25). We must also understand that the rising of the fallen ones, that is, the corresponding return of the unbelievers, is also a reality. And for those who fell, their fall was no different than that of Adam and Eve. But the punishment is not the same for those who did not believe the announcement before the coming of the Lord, as for those who remain in their unbelief after the Lord has come and revealed His teaching (cf. Acts 11:30). Indeed, this is what the Lord means when He says: *This gospel of the kingdom will be preached in all the world as a witness to all the nations, and then the end will come* (Mt. 24:14). This is what will condemn the unbelievers and put them to shame. For after having heard the teaching and the testimony, they deserve even greater punishment (cf. Lk. 12:47). But especially in the case of the people of Israel, their transgression was even greater. This is why He left them no freedom to act like He did the other nations, and so all that they had of value was lost to them and destroyed; they were punished even more harshly than those nations who had remained in unbelief (cf. Mt. 11:20-24). And this is because they did not receive Him whom the Prophets foretold, but the fools considered the righteous and longsuffering One an evildoer, and in their unbelief, they became the murderers of Christ (cf. 1 Cor. 2:8). And in exchange for their unbelief, their city was destroyed, and their people were wiped out and exiled, and every noble and precious thing they had was obliterated (cf. Mt. 22:1-14). But the believers He received into the true 'rising' or 'resurrection', for they were freed of the yoke and bondage of the ancient Law (cf. Mt. 28:30); they were buried with

Christ through Baptism and rose together with Him (cf. Rom. 6:4-5, 8) and given eternal life.

Certain Fathers would add that the Lord did not come 'for the fall' of some 'and the rising' of others, for it was not He who was responsible for the fall, for they themselves chose to fall, while the others chose to rise. Rather, some fall because of the evil that they chose, while others rise because of the good that they chose (cf. Jas. 1:13-14). For indeed, if the wicked ones who oppress us did not fall by afflicting the good, then the good among us would never be made manifest (cf. Rom. 11:11-12). If unbelief did not fall, then belief could not rise. If the sin of afflicting righteousness did not fall, then righteousness could not rise up and manifest itself among us, as the Apostle Paul says: *When I am weak, then I am strong* (2 Cor. 12:10). He himself was frail and yet strong; frail in body, but strong in the Spirit. In this way the power of Christ draws the believers to rise up through falling; that is, that they should fall as regards heard-heartedness and the barrenness of sins, and rise up to the resurrection of righteousness. *This Child is destined for the fall and rising of many in Israel, and* upon the cross He will be declared to be *a sign which will be spoken against* (Lk. 2:34), for he will be the giver of crowns and condemnation (cf. Rev. 2:10). This cross is the crown for those of us who believe in Christ, a sign of our salvation and a seal of our King; but it is *spoken against*, for while some are inclined to the cross, others hate and revile it, yet the believers love it and venerate it with faith and reverence. Moreover, Christ Himself is called *a sign that will be spoken against*, for it was He who worked supernatural wonders; He was accepted by some who believed that He did His miracles by the Holy Spirit, while others, wicked and vile, blasphemed Him and claimed that He did them *by Beelzebub, the ruler of the demons* (Mt. 12:24), and testified all kinds of other things against Him (cf. Mk. 14:56). Some even said that He did not come in the body, others said that His incarnation was only an appearance, while still others claimed that he took on human flesh, but not a human mind. These are the opinions of senseless fools. Indeed, the slanderers who *resist the truth* (2 Tim. 3:8) have started many and various rumors.

All that we have said until now concerning this, and all that we are now discussing, is what Simeon means by 'a sign that will be spoken against'. The elder addressed to the Virgin all the words of this prophecy concerning herself and her son and King, for he knew that anything pertaining to her Son the blessed Virgin would see as pertaining to herself. This is why he did not only mention pleasant things, but also sorrowful things, so that when they came to pass, the blessed Virgin would remember the prophecy and be comforted. This is why he said: *A sword will pierce your own soul also* (Lk. 2:35). And indeed, a sword did pierce the soul of His blessed mother when His Passion was at hand. How sorely was her heart afflicted when she beheld her Son's suffering! The holy Fathers speak also of the power of this word: A 'sword' is a word that tries and judges the thoughts, *piercing even to the division of soul and spirit, and of joints and marrow, and is a discerner of the thoughts and intents of the heart* (Heb. 4:12). Thus, during the Passion of the Christ, every soul passed through judgment, just as the Lord said: *All of you will be made to stumble because of Me* (Mk. 14:27). So Simeon speaks of this to the holy Virgin Mary: "When you stand before the Cross and see your Son's suffering and hear Him cry, *Eli, Eli, lama sabachthani?* (Mt. 27:46; cf. Ps. 21:2), and, *Father, into Your hands I commit my spirit* (Lk. 23:46; cf. Ps. 30:6), and when He says, *I am thirsty*, and they bring Him sour wine (Jn. 19:28; cf. Ps. 68:22), and *when Jesus receives the sour wine, says, "It is finished!" And bowing His head, He gives up His spirit* (Jn. 19:30), and you hear and see these things and other dreadful words and deeds like them, and all this after the annunciation of Gabriel, after the ineffable birth, which you yourself experienced, and even after seeing the glorious miracles, your soul will be gripped with anguish. But in spite of all this, it is better for the merciful Lord *to taste death* (cf. Heb. 2:9) for the sake of the whole world, and to justify the whole world by His blood (cf. Rom. 5:9).

"I am saying these things to your very soul," says the elder. "For it has more understanding than any other; the Lord's testing, which will grieve you, is the 'sword' which will reveal the thoughts of all men (cf. Lk. 2:35)." He goes on to mention the anguish and doubts that will overwhelm the Apostles at Christ's crucifixion, which will cut Mary's pure heart to the quick. But immediately afterwards will follow the healing and comfort from the Lord, which will strengthen their hearts with His consolation, so as to reveal His power (cf. Lk. 21:31-32). This is surely the meaning of the verse: *that the thoughts of many hearts may be revealed.* For when the Lord's Passion was accomplished on the cross and the mystery of our salvation was complete, the thoughts of many were indeed revealed, those that each harbored about the person of the Christ, whether they were faith and love or deception and hatred; for some clearly ridiculed and delighted in His crucifixion, but these are not his primary, sworn enemies; while others accept the love that was revealed at the Passion with hypocrisy, even before those who have good thoughts and a good will. Yet still others suffered with Him and mourned and confessed the Lord upon the cross, like the one robber (cf. Lk. 23:40-43), *that the thoughts of many hearts may be revealed.* And many of them who stumbled at first, once they had recovered their strength after the Savior's resurrection, believed and were illuminated by the grace of Christ.

But let us now return to our subject. After they had arrived at the temple and been received by the expectant Simeon, the prophetic words and the doxology of Anna, *when they had performed all things according to the law of the Lord, they returned to Galilee, to their own city, Nazareth* (Lk. 2:39), according to the Gospel of Luke. Then the angel of the Lord appeared to Joseph and told him to flee to Egypt, according to the Gospel of Matthew (cf. Mt. 2:13). This newborn babe, the uncreated God Himself, arranged everything. With His consent, they fled to Egypt, both His mother and Joseph. And just afterwards the children were slaughtered by the wicked Herod. At that time, John the great Forerunner of the Savior had a desire; for he who had seen *the true Light* (cf. Jn. 1:9) and leapt with joy even before he had been born and seen the visible light; while he was still in his mother's womb, he was appointed herald before he could speak, and before he had formed a single word he had borne witness to the Word (cf. Lk. 1:41; Jn. 1:6-9). John desired to taste death and receive the crown of martyrdom, just like the other children; for his house and line were descended from Bethlehem and its surrounding country. And while he had been born six months earlier, the ruler's evil decree had ordered all the newborns younger or slightly older than two years in Bethlehem and its surrounding country to be put to death, so that the One they were looking for would have no means of escape. But God the Lord whom they were trying to murder was watching over the great Forerunner and Baptizer, and His divine providence had helped Him to escape to Egypt. It was He who shielded His Forerunner, lest he be slain together with the newborns, but when he had come of age, he should be His testimony, and His forerunner to those who dwell in Hades, to preach to them His deliverance. But He who came into the world on our behalf, by His great mercy, saved Elizabeth and her son from the hand of those who would murder them. So the relative of the Theotokos in flesh and in spirit fled with her son into the desert and cried out to the mountain: "O mountain of God! Receive a mother and her child!" And the mountain received them and hid them, as the Lord had commanded. There Elizabeth left her son John and died. So just as all these things, the conception and birth of the *Sun of Righteousness* (cf. Mal. 4:2), *the Bridegroom* of the Church (cf. Eph. 5:22-33; Rev. 21:9), are ineffable, so too in the case of His minister; he who is called *the lamp* for *the Light* (Jn. 5:35; cf. Jn. 1:7) and *the voice* of the Lord (Mt. 3:3; Is. 40:3), *the friend of the Bridegroom* (Jn. 3:29) and *the Forerunner* of the Lord (cf. Lk. 1:17). His rise and way of life are inexpressible, how he survived and found food *in the desert till the day of his manifestation to Israel* (cf. Lk. 1:80). But the ungodly murderers of the newborns, when they failed to apprehend Elizabeth and her son John, they turned and vented their rage against his father Zachariah, and by order of the vile Herod, they slew him in the blessed place, while he was ministering in the temple and standing before the altar, bringing sacrificial gifts before God (cf. Mt. 23:35). And thus he discharged his service.

Meanwhile, when the newborn child, the King of all things, departed for Egypt, he drove out the demons of Egypt (cf. Is. 19:1) and destroyed every deception, for all who live there are idol-worshipers, more enslaved to the demons than any other nation (cf. 1 Cor. 10:20). There were many sorcerers (cf. Ex. 7:11), *inventors of every evil* (Rom. 1:29), but even the other Egyptians were truly more enslaved to the worship of idols and detestable serpents (cf. Wis. 11:15) and the trees of the earth. The offered sacrifices to the heifer and honored her as a god, calling her "Apis"; likewise they had made a god of the goat. They sacrificed also to cats and mice and worshipped the crocodile, the monster of the Nile River. They worshipped garlic and onion (cf. Num. 11:5) and other hideous and awful creatures and plants. The sorcerers served the demons as guardians of the air (cf. Eph. 2:2), they summoned them and observed the stars to whom they sacrificed, and interpreted omens and practiced divination (cf. Gen. 44:5). Both the sorcerers and the common idolaters who had gone so miserably astray, Christ rescued from their great delusion by His coming into the world. The enemy saw the cascade of the Savior's miracles and realized that their hearts had now been captivated even more by Christ than by himself of old. In fact, at His birth, the Savior summoned to Himself the sorcerers of Persia and so broke every illusion of the demons, the rulers of the air, and every delusion of astrology and magic. And He Himself went down to

Egypt as a man soon after, together with his purest mother, and destroyed all the Egyptian impurity, driving out all the snakes and scorpions of Egypt (cf. Ex. 7:12) and dispelling the gloom of destruction (cf. Ex. 10:21). So His mother watched her countrymen and the inhabitants of Judea become enemies and persecutors, while the enemies and foreigners of Egypt she found to be fast friends. So she forsook Judea and settled in Egypt. Thus the Egyptians saw and experienced what had been said long before by the Prophet Isaiah: God in the flesh with His immaculate mother (Is. 19:1).

Our Lord Jesus Christ and His most holy mother remained in Egypt, as the Fathers tell us, for two years. After that, the wicked Herod died of a frightful illness, and once again, *an angel of the Lord appeared in a dream to Joseph in Egypt, saying, "Arise, take the young Child and His mother, and go to the land of Israel, for those who sought the young Child's life are dead." Then he arose, took the young Child and His mother, and came into the land of Israel* [...] *and, being warned by God in a dream, he turned aside into the region of Galilee. And he came and dwelt in a city called Nazareth, that it might be fulfilled which was spoken by the prophets*: first, that *He shall be called a Nazarene*, and second, *Out of Egypt I called my Son* (Mt. 2:15, 19-23). So we see that Jesus went down into Egypt, returned from there and settled in Nazareth because of the appearance and the words of the angel, according to the Gospel of Matthew.

If someone were to say that the Gospel of Luke makes no mention of the angelic vision and the return to Nazareth, we would remind him that it clearly records that after the Lord's presentation at the temple, *when they had performed all things according to the law of the Lord, they returned to Galilee, to their own city, Nazareth* (Lk. 2:39). So there is no discrepancy between the two blessed Evangelists. Luke reports the events *before* going down to Egypt, for his account mostly covers the journey to Bethlehem in Judea, and the Lord's supernatural birth that followed. They remained there in Bethlehem for forty days, whereupon they took the baby Jesus to Jerusalem to be purified according to the Law of the Lord, where the elder Simeon took Him into his arms. When all this had come to pass, they returned home to the city of Nazareth, where they had been living, all in accordance with the Lord's foreknowledge and ordination, who took on flesh from the Virgin for the redemption of mankind. After Jesus had turned two years old in Nazareth, as the Fathers tell us, the angel of the Lord appeared to Joseph and instructed him to flee to Egypt, for Herod was plotting to come and search for the newborn King and put Him to death. So after they had spent two years in Egypt, the wicked Herod died, and the angel of the Lord appeared to Joseph and instructed him to return to the land of Israel: *Then he arose, took the young Child and His mother, and came into the land of Israel. But when he heard that Archelaus was reigning over Judea instead of his father Herod, he was afraid to go there. And being warned by God in a dream, he turned aside* [...] *And he came and dwelt in a city called Nazareth* (Mt. 2:21-23). [110]

O how great and wonderful is the all-pure and blessed mother! How many tears and toils did she meet with from the beginning until the end, even though all those afflictions she encountered were mingled with the consolation of the Lord. For indeed, after the annunciation of Gabriel and her unspeakable conception, Joseph was plagued by doubts, as the Gospel says: *He was minded to put her away secretly* (Mt. 1:19). How these doubts must have tortured and distressed and afflicted his holy soul! But the angel's appearance put all doubts to rest, for he informed him that Mary had conceived by the Holy Spirit and that this birth would be the salvation of the whole world. The time for the blessed birth came, together with the decree from the Emperor that they must go up to Bethlehem in Judea. So they departed from Nazareth in Galilee and with great effort and hardship they reached Judea. Now, when they arrived in Bethlehem, the time came for the Virgin to give birth, and the immaculate one brought into the world her Son, the Lord of all, *and wrapped Him in swaddling cloths, and laid Him in a manger, because there was no room for them in the inn* (Lk. 2:7). But all their time there was in fact spent in penury and want. But even here, their afflictions were joined with consolations: the messages and glorification of the angels, the shepherds' setting out in search for the confirmation of the Child's birth, the proclamation of all the angelic messages concerning Him, as well as all that they themselves observed, left them astonished and magnifying God. At the same time the wisemen arrived, led by the star, and venerated the child, the King of all and his most holy mother, bringing Him the precious gifts. And finally, they went up to Jerusalem and presented the child at the temple, which defies expression or comprehension, where He was received by Simeon, who ultimately spoke a blessing and a prophecy over Him.

Sometime after these consolations, Herod the foolish rogue appeared and forced the most holy mother to flee to Egypt with her beloved Son, the King of all. Again they endured afflictions, penury, hardships, and fears as Herod sought the child's life. He who had given being to every *living soul* (cf. Gen. 2:7) and had come to seek the lost sheep (cf. Lk. 15:6) and the lost drachma (cf. Lk. 15:9), which bears the image of the King (cf. Lk. 20:24; Gen 1:26).

So He left Egypt; He who of old had led His fugitive people out of Egypt and guided them through the sea on dry land, "without getting their feet wet" (cf. Ex. 13:17-14:29). He continued to preserve His people Israel from all evils, and now they were persecuting Him and seeking His life. The Lord, the Ruler of all things visible and invisible, fled into exile in a foreign land, moving from place to place with His blessed mother. She bravely endured all these trials and hardships of the fragile nature of woman, for she bore the infant in her arms, the God who was before all the ages. And all these things were forecasts and symbols of the redemption, as well as the longsuffering of the holy Virgin, as her life and wisdom up to this point had taught her, constantly growing in the holy purity of her virginity.

When after all these things the mother of God returned from Egypt with Joseph and her beloved Son, they finally and with much toil reached the promised land (cf. Gen. 12:7). The supremely blessed mother learned that that tyrant who had sought to destroy her holy Child had met the utterly wretched demise he so rightfully deserved. First, he had put his wife to death, brutally and without cause, together with his children and his whole household. He was then murdered himself most heinously, and thus ended his wretched life. His kingdom was split into four realms by law. And once Archelaus had taken his place (this being the only one of his family who had survived, since he had not managed to slay all his sons), Joseph received the angel's instruction. So he went and settled in the city of Nazareth and did not depart for Judea, for the very same angel had warned him about this that had told them to flee to Egypt for the same reason. He told Joseph not to go up to Judea now, but said: *Arise, take the young Child and His mother, and go to the land of Israel, for those who sought the young Child's life are dead* (Mt. 2:20).

One object of study for those who are interested, however, is this: Archelaus was king while Pilate ruled Judea. But we must note that during the time of Christ's incarnation and just before, the kingdom of the Hebrews and their high priesthood had passed into the hands of the Romans, as the Prophet says: *A ruler shall not fail from Judah* [...] *until there come the things stored up for him* (Gen. 49:10). This is the reason why Aristobulus was the high priest and king; he had a younger brother named Hyrcanus, who so hated his brother Aristobulus that he declared war on him and put him in dire straits. The Roman governor Pompey had Aristobulus sent to Rome in chains and forced the chief priests of Jerusalem to pay tribute to Rome. Sometime later, Herod was appointed vassal king of Judea and enjoyed the financial and military support of Emperor Augustus. He was called "king", but in reality he was a slave, for he had no authority even over his own children. Without the Emperor's approval, he was powerless. Now, after the death of Herod, the Hebrews sank into even more abject slavery to the Romans. While Herod was still alive, the decree went out from Caesar Augustus for the entire empire to be registered. All the Jews were marked down as slaves, and the Roman governor ratified the registration, as the Gospel says: *This census first took place while Quirinius was governing Syria* (Lk. 2:2). This census authorized the administrators, judges, soldiers and defenders of the land: all Romans, so that the Hebrews would have no chance to revolt, since all the power and dominion now belonged to the Romans. So in this way, the Emperor awarded the kingdom of Judea to whomever he pleased, though the one appointed king did not have the power of that office but was fully subjugated to the emperor. This is why the governor under King Archelaus was Pilate, while later the younger Herod (Antipas), son of the other Herod (the Great), would hand our Lord Jesus Christ over to the Hebrews to be crucified. Pilate was the governor, and Herod the Tetrarch was passing through Jerusalem at that time. It is common knowledge that the power and the authority of the Emperor rested with the Roman governors. But let us return and continue our topic.

Now, the holy Gospel says: *Jesus increased in wisdom and stature, and in favor with God and men* (Lk. 2:52). These words refer not to His deity, but to that which was not already perfect in the beginning and not yet revealed to Him who was perfect and beyond all perfection and stood firmer than any constancy and was full of every good thing. But the Gospel speaks of the gradual growth of His human nature, the development of His physical strength. On closer study of the words used here, we uncover their meaning: *Jesus increased in wisdom and stature and in favor*. Indeed, the increase in wisdom and stature and favor does not refer to His deity, for that was already full from the beginning and lacked nothing; and it is pointless to speculate about whether he was humanly speaking more gifted than others or if He had more gifts of the Holy Spirit who dwelled in Him. For from the very beginning He possessed all grace, and from the moment His two natures were united, he possessed *all the fullness of the Godhead bodily* (Col. 2:9), as the Apostle Paul says. But this phrase 'increased in wisdom and stature and favor' means that, as soon as the divine nature was joined with the human nature and dwelled in Him, he was immediately filled with grace and wisdom that manifested and shone forth all the more as he developed physically and grew in stature. He received no additional grace and wisdom, but the fullness of grace and wisdom were made manifest by His miraculous powers and it became clear (as the Apostle says), that *He is before all things, and in Him all things consist.* [...] *For it pleased the Father that in Him all the fullness should dwell, and by Him to reconcile all things to Himself* (Col. 7:17, 19-20). But it was unbefitting that He should display His wisdom before reaching a certain age, but since our nature cannot express itself articulately until it is twelve years old, He Himself also saw fit to wait until His twelfth year of physical development.

Now, during the same feast on which the Hebrews would later arrest Him out of envy and betray Him to His passion, *and when He* (His human nature) *was twelve years old, they went up to Jerusalem according to the custom of the feast. When they had finished the days, as they returned, the Boy Jesus lingered behind in Jerusalem* (Lk. 2:42-43) without His parents' noticing, neither His mother who had truly given birth to Him, nor Joseph, who was His father in name only; in fact, no one knew anything at all. And consider why he lingered behind without their knowledge: It was so that they would not keep Him from staying in the city, and He would not have to appear disobedient. For once he remained in Jerusalem, He went to the temple and took His seat among the teachers, instructed and taught the teachers and the priests; but not with authority (cf. Mt. 7:29) or arrogance, He who was the single spring of all wisdom and knowledge (cf. Col. 2:3), who gives to all reason and wisdom. But He did this in consideration of His own age and the honor he was due, and thus he yielded His seat to another. He gave the seat of honor to the priests and the teachers, so that they could instruct and teach the people, while He Himself posed brilliant questions, listened with understanding, and answered decisively. All *were astonished at His understanding* and wisdom (Lk. 2:47), for He was truly astonishing.

Meanwhile, His most holy mother together with Joseph *sought Him among their relatives and acquaintances. So when they did not find Him, they returned to Jerusalem, seeking Him. Now so it was that after three days they found Him in the temple, sitting in the midst of the teachers, both listening to them and asking them questions. And all who heard Him were astonished at His understanding and answers* [...] *His mother said to Him, "Son, why have You done this to us? Look, Your father and I have sought You anxiously."* (Lk. 2:45-48). Then the blessed, dearest Lord helped His mother grasp the reality and recognize His true Father, and told them not to see Him merely as human but as God incarnate, for His father's house (that is, the temple) is also His own (cf. Mt. 21:13; Jn. 14:2); just as everything in His Father's possession belongs likewise to the Son, and those who deny this are clearly misguided and can never expect to understand the full truth. This is why He says to them: *"Why did you seek Me? Did you not know that I must be about My Father's business?"* (Lk. 2:49). In this holy place He declared for the first time with clarity and godlike dignity His divine origin, and for them to wonder whether His Father is God, then He as the Son must be of the same nature with the Father, for the Father and the Son are of one single nature, as He Himself states elsewhere: *He who has seen Me has seen the Father*. He further tells His disciples: *If you had known Me, you would have known My Father also; and from now on you know Him and have seen Him* (Jn. 14:9, 7). As He also said to the Jews: *If you had known Me, you would have known My Father also* (Jn. 8:19).

So this was the first manifestation and the first teaching in which the wisdom and power of the boy Jesus were so divinely and splendidly revealed. His mother also was astonished, Joseph and all who were present, even though they could not fully comprehend the power of His words (Lk. 2:50). *Then He went down with them and came to Nazareth, and was subject to them, but His mother kept all these things in her heart* (Lk. 2:51), as the holy Gospel says. *And Jesus increased in wisdom and stature, and in favor with God and men* (Lk. 2:52). During this whole time, from then until His baptism, He passed without any display of His power to work miracles. But we should note here that the book which speaks of the childhood of Christ should not be taken into consideration, for it was never taken into the canon of the Church and stands in conflict with the words of the holy Evangelists. This book contends against the truth, for it was concocted by some careless weaver of fairy tales. Luke the Evangelist preaches the Gospel truth concisely and with caution, saying that *Jesus increased in wisdom and stature, and in favor with God and men*, as we have already noted in our comment on this passage. And He truly was full of wisdom and grace, the very wellspring of wisdom and grace, the desire of all rational and mindful men; furthermore, he was comely of body, *more beautiful than the sons of men* (Ps. 44:3), as the Prophet says; He had perfect proportions, fine features and a good height, he was kind and serene in His conversation. And all of His life He was filled with the grace of the Holy Spirit. Just as with all the other good things, so also in conversation and his comportment was exemplary, a paragon of every virtue; His meekness and mildness were incomparable and indescribable.

A razor shall not come upon his head (Num. 6:5; Jud. 13:5). He did not let any man serve Him (cf. Mk. 10:45), except His holy and most-blessed mother; and until His baptism he did not preach. But in reality, His whole behavior reveals that His life and behavior were examples and lessons in virtue. For all that He taught His disciples and the people after His baptism were things that He Himself had practiced assiduously from His childhood until His death. And when I say "practiced", I mean according to the convention and nature and measures of men, for God cannot be confined by the bounds of human conventions of behavior, for He is incomparably superior to all creation, from everlasting to everlasting, as the Prophet David says: *You are from everlasting to everlasting* (Ps. 89:2). But through His nature and substance, the flesh that He had received from the Virgin Mary, He practiced every virtue in deed and every precept of the Law that had been laid down by the mouth of Moses. No one else could fulfill the Law in its entirety without bending it, except for Jesus who took on flesh for our salvation and showed us what it means to love God and men (cf. 1 Jn. 3:16), and what is mercy, grace and gentleness, peace, humility and patience, reverence and obedience of parents, fasting, prayer. The blessed One exemplified every virtue to men, both in deed, and later in word. This gave His holy mother the chance to become the disciple of her dearest Son, the true mother of Wisdom, for she no longer saw him as men see, or as a man only, but served Him with reverence as God and took His words like the oracles of God. Thus, she forgot none of His words and deeds, as the Gospel says: *His mother kept all these things in her heart*, awaiting the time of its fulfillment. She treasured up His words and deeds within her, according to His order and plan of salvation, as further assurances and forecasts of the unspeakable mysteries and wonders to come. But the Gospel does not mention anything that followed, so we will not mention it either, just as He Himself, the Word of God made flesh for our salvation, did not give any sign to show the power of His divinity before he had attained physical maturity and reached the point when His foreknowledge had decided to be revealed. This would take place with the display of His wonders and His life-giving passion, which were both revealed at once, for they are intimately connected. For the miracles were guarantees of His preaching, and the preaching the subject of His miracles; these two drew innumerable crowds, who gathered to see His miracles and hear His teaching. They won him the envy of the chief priests and the pharisees. This is why they opposed him and delivered Him over to His passion; and so the mystery of the Divine Economy was fulfilled.

V: THE MANIFESTATION OF DIVINITY

Let us now discuss the baptism and manifestation of the divinity of the Lord. Jesus was already thirty years old, or somewhat more (cf. Lk. 3:23). Then, *in the fifteenth year of the reign of Tiberius Caesar* [...] *the word of God came to John the son of Zacharias in the wilderness. And he went into all the region around the Jordan, preaching a baptism of repentance for the remission of sins* (Lk. 3:1, 2). *Then Jerusalem, all Judea, and all the region around the Jordan went out to him and were baptized by him in the Jordan, confessing their sins* (Mt. 3:5-6), for his conduct was supernatural and admired by all; this is why they gathered around him listened to his teaching, and were baptized by him. But all these things came to pass in accordance with Divine providence. For his name had to be spread so that his preaching and testimony about our Lord Jesus Christ could be believed. This is why he preached, saying: *I indeed baptize you with water unto repentance, but He who is coming after me is mightier than I, whose sandals I am not worthy to carry. He will baptize you with the Holy Spirit and fire* (Mt. 3:11). *Then Jesus came from Nazareth in Galilee to John at the Jordan to be baptized by him* (cf. Mt. 3:13; Mk. 1:7-11). *When He had been baptized, Jesus came up immediately from the water; and behold, the heavens were opened to Him, and He saw the Spirit of God descending like a dove and alighting upon Him. And suddenly a voice came from heaven, saying, "This is My beloved Son, in whom I am well pleased"* (Mt. 3:16-17).

These are the great mysteries that His brilliant witness was proclaiming. For this reason the Lord exalted John and praised him before the people - so that his witness would be accepted. And thus, many believed his word and became disciples of the Lord, such as Andrew, Peter, and John, who wrote: *Again, the next day, John (the Forerunner) stood with two of his disciples* (Jn. 1:35). These were Andrew (Jn. 1:41) and John the Evangelist. *And looking at Jesus as He walked, he said, "Behold the Lamb of God!" The two disciples heard him speak, and they followed Jesus* (Jn. 1:36-37). And many others believed based on the testimony of John, for he was admired by all for his way of life, his strange diet, his simple attire, and his fearless preaching, to the extent that they *reasoned in their hearts about John, whether he was the Christ or not* (Lk. 3:15). So the Jews sent priests and Levites from Jerusalem to ask him who he is. He confessed: *I am not the Christ* [...] *but there stands One among you whom you do not know. It is He who, coming after me, is before me, whose sandal strap I am not worthy to loose* (Jn. 1:20, 26-27). But what do these words mean? "He must come after me, He existed before me, and stands among you"? Meaning He will come after him as regards His preaching, for John was the first to begin preaching, and only later the Lord Jesus. John appeared first, respected by all, and then the Lord Jesus followed, even though He was before him in divine honor and glory, for it is natural for the Forerunner to announce and point to the coming King. And so He is among you, for He came and was baptized just like you all. But the Baptist acknowledged Him not only with words, but even pointed to Him with his finger when he saw Jesus coming to him: *Behold! The Lamb of God who takes away the sin of the world!* (Jn. 1:29). Not because He had any need of purification, but because He brought the purification of the whole world. This is why John made such an effort to draw attention to Him and said, *"This is He of whom I said, 'After me comes a Man who is preferred before me, for He was before me.' I did not know Him; but that He should be revealed to Israel, therefore I came baptizing with water." And John bore witness, saying, "I saw the Spirit descending from heaven like a dove, and He remained upon Him. I did not know Him, but He who sent me to baptize with water said to me, 'Upon whom you see the Spirit descending, and remaining on Him, this is He who baptizes with the Holy Spirit.' And I have seen and testified that this is the Son of God"* (Jn. 1:30-34).

Now, of course the Holy Spirit did not only remain on Him only at that time or at the exact moment when the Forerunner was watching. How could this be the case for Him in whom *dwells all the fulness of the Godhead* from the very beginning (cf. Col. 2:9)? But the Holy Spirit was seen by the Baptist in the form of a dove in order to manifest to all Him who is the true Son of God and true God Himself. And I believe that, just as He worked many miracles as signs for our sake, so also, He did this sign for our sake, as the Holy Spirit came down at His baptism (cf. Jn. 12:30). Thus He displayed the coming of the Holy Spirit, and at the same time the Father's voice was heard testifying to the Lord Jesus: *This is My beloved Son, in whom I am well pleased* (Mt. 3:17).

And thus there was revealed in the Jordan the unified Holy Trinity, joined in nature and distinct in persons: three persons, for each has a unique name. The Son appears in the flesh in the Jordan River, the Spirit descends on Him as a dove, and the Father bears witness from on high about His beloved Son. And so the three persons of the one Godhead were revealed. And moreover the Father's testimony is to show us that the nature of the God-man Christ is one, that God deified the nature of man by becoming man. This is why the Father calls Him who is two natures, divine and human, united in one person, His 'beloved Son'.

Now, only John was found worthy to see the Holy Spirit. But the voice and the Father's testimony was heard by all the people, as on Mt. Sinai of old, when God gave His Law to Moses (cf. Ex. 19:16-25). Only Moses saw the vision, while the people only heard the voice; and not even all who were present heard the voice, but only those who were found worthy. Those who were unworthy were excluded from hearing the voice and coming under the Law. And so, both were necessary and right (cf. Mt. 3:15) for Christ's baptism. For if the people were just as worthy as John, then they would have likewise been permitted to see the Holy Spirit and hear the voice of the Father, and He would not have accorded greater honor to John the Baptist and the Forerunner, and the vision of the fearsome and magnificent descent of the Holy Spirit would have been shared by all. On the other hand, if the people had not heard any voice at all, then the testimony about the Christ would have not been made known, and they would have doubted John's testimony and claimed he was testifying to what he did not know or showing favoritism to Jesus. But since the voice was heard by all the people, it gave John's testimony credibility and caused everyone to understand the glory of the Lord Jesus.

After His baptism, *Jesus was led up by the Spirit into the wilderness* (Mt. 4:1) to a remote place, in order for the warrior to gather His strength for battle and to go before us by showing us the way of all believers after baptism: fasting and struggle. He fasted for forty days, and *afterward He was hungry* (Mt. 4:2), due to His bodily nature. The devil appeared and tested Him in many ways, and the Lord Jesus defeated him in pitched battle and beat him into retreat. After His victory, *angels came and ministered to Him* (Mt. 4:11). This is clearly a message for us that, once we have believed and been baptized, we possess the resources to withstand temptations, and after the temptation, the reward and grace is apportioned to the contestants.

Jesus returned to the place where John had been. John announced Him on sight, as he had done before; not once, but two times. That is when the disciples of John the Baptist, Andrew and John (cf. Jn.

1:37), who were the first to come, by virtue of their good choice. For Andrew was a paragon of courage, and John was a paragon of purity. Andrew led his firstborn brother Peter to Jesus as a disciple; the second-born thus led the firstborn to spiritual birth, and in this birth, Peter was not the firstborn. From then on, John entrusted his disciples to Christ the King, just as he had entrusted his testimony about Him to them. He himself was thrown into prison a short time later by Herod, for John desired to be a Forerunner likewise of the Passion of Jesus, just as he had been the Forerunner both of His preaching and His baptism. What does the holy Gospel tell us on this count? *Now when Jesus heard that John had been put in prison, He departed to Galilee* [...] *From that time Jesus began to preach and to say, "Repent, for the kingdom of heaven is at hand"* (Mt. 4:12, 17). He began preaching and teaching in Galilee. There He took Philip and Nathanael as His disciples (cf. Jn. 1:44-48), after having initially called Peter, Andrew, James, and John.

Two days later, *there was a wedding in Cana of Galilee*, and there He produced His first miracle: changing water into wine. His immaculate and most-holy mother was there as well, an eye-witness of the Lord's miracles and a hearer of His preaching. This is why she, the cause of all good, was the mediator of His first miracle; for she was His most-holy mother and desired to see the signs of her Son and Lord. This is why she drew His attention with reverence and understanding to the wine; she did not command Him to perform a miracle, but merely tactfully informed Him of the precarious situation: *They have no wine*. Her heart's desire was to see Him work a miracle, for she knew that He was the Creator of all things and Renewer of creation (cf. Rev. 21:5). He who would transform all things according to His will and had supernaturally taken up residence in her womb while preserving her virginity intact. He had emerged from her womb as He saw fit; not opening it but keeping it sealed. The blessed Virgin had perceived that He could do whatever He wanted, so she gently directed His attention to the situation at hand. He, the patient One, her Lord and Son, in order to teach greater humility and reverence before Him, for the power of His divinity must be revealed even more, merely admonished her with the words: *Woman, what does your concern have to do with Me? My hour has not yet come* (Jn. 2:4). But indeed, He consented to fulfilling her request. He honored her as His mother and fulfilled her heart's desire. The blessed Virgin knew well His goodness and power. This is why she said to the servants: *Whatever He says to you, do it.* And indeed, the ineffable power of the Lord changed the water into choicest wine. But the transformation of water into wine also caused a like transformation in him who had invited Jesus to the wedding. The bridegroom left the wedding and the house, and followed and ministered to the highest Overseer, the blessed King and Lord, the Bridegroom of holy and spotless souls. The bride also followed suit, and thereafter became a handmaiden of the most-holy mother of the Lord. And so the Lord's miracle did not only transform the water into wine, but also the wedding into virginity. From that time on, the most-holy Virgin and mother of the Lord clove even closer to her blessed Lord and beloved Son, as much as she could. Wherever He went, she followed Him and considered it the light of her bodily eyes and the eyes of her soul to travel with Him and hear His words.

And when the Lord went to Peter's house and healed his mother-in-law who *lay sick with a fever* (cf. Mk. 1:29-31), His most-holy and favored Mother the Virgin Mary was with Him, as well as the women who had become His disciples. From then on Peter's mother-in-law and her daughter, Peter's wife, followed the Lord's preaching and travelled together with the Mother of God. They became her handmaidens and waited on her.

Then the Lord Jesus once again left Nazareth together with His holy mother, for Joseph, with whom the holy Virgin had once been betrothed, had finished the course of this fleeting life, old and full of years, having reached the age of one hundred and ten. He who had been found worthy to support and care for Jesus Christ, the Lord and King of all things, and had been an eyewitness to the inexpressible mysteries of His birth and maturation, and (after His baptism) of His miracles. So he entered into eternal life and received from the Lord Jesus Christ a blessing worthy of his faithful support and service. The sons of Joseph, James and Jude, followed Jesus as disciples; his daughters were companions of the holy Mother of God. On all of the Lord's journeys when he preached the gospel of salvation and healed every illness, both acute and chronic, they followed Him at all times, serving Him and witnessing His miracles, as is written in the holy Gospel: There were *many women who followed Jesus from Galilee, ministering to Him* (Mt. 27:55). But the holy and glorious Mother of God was always their leader; she interceded with her Son and Lord on their behalf and passed on His instructions.

From there the One who seeks salvation for all passed on to the Sea of Galilee, which was great and renowned, brimming with fish in its depths and surrounded on all sides with countless plants of all shapes and sizes. There he told Peter to launch out to fish after He had finished preaching to the people from within the boat. They cast their nets and caught such a great quantity of fish that they *were astonished at the catch of fish which they had taken; and so also were James and John, the sons of Zebedee, who were partners with Simon. And Jesus said to Simon, "Do not be afraid. From now on you will catch men." So when they had brought their boats to land, they forsook all and followed Him* (Lk. 5:9-11). They had followed Him before, but this time it was decisive.

From the Sea of Galilee, the Lord went on to Capernaum, where He healed the paralytic (who was a pattern of our own decrepit and crippled nature); for as the man stretched his limbs, Jesus commanded him to take up his bed and go to his house (cf. Mt. 9:1-8), just as He who is great in mercy restored our fallen nature and gathered our shattered members together in faith (that is, the scattered nations) and made us into one body in submission to the Head of all, our Christ and God Himself. He commanded us to carry the yoke of His commandments (cf. Mt. 11:29) and to return to our ancestral homeland, the Paradise from whence we fell. And the people gathered in droves to behold the countless miracles of the Lord, so many that the Gospel writers could not write them all down, for *if they were written one by one, I suppose that even the world itself could not contain the books that would be written* (Jn. 21:25). Indeed, the mind of worldly men cannot contain such a wondrous multitude and power.

So the Lord taught the people and healed their infirmities, not only of the body, but of the soul as well. And the disciples taught those who had been taught and led to the faith, baptizing them as the Lord commanded (cf. Jn. 4:2). For just as the Lord fulfilled all the precepts of the ancient Law first before instituting the new Law (cf. Mt. 5:17), in the same way He Himself received John's baptism in the Jordan river, and then brought about His own baptism with the gift of the Holy Spirit, commanding His disciples to keep it just as He had shown them (cf. Mt. 28:18-20).

At that time, Zebedee, the father of James and John, died, and they asked the Lord to go and bury their father, but He who is rich in mercy did not permit them, that they might learn not to desire anything more than being with Him. And they obeyed His commandment, forsaking their own will. But then He commanded them to go and care for their house and their mother. They went and offered up the best they had, they brought their mother and added her to the number of the attendants of the holy Mother of God, to serve the Lord of all things together with her. They distributed a portion of their inheritance among the poor, as the Lord commanded, and donated another portion for the other disciples to use, and the rest they sold and bought the house of Zion, where the Mother of the Lord would live after His crucifixion and ascension. That is where the Beloved Disciple took her after the Lord committed her to his care while He was on the cross, and settled her there and cared for her, as the dearest King had commanded.

By now, Judea as well as Galilee was full of the wonders and signs of Christ; His mother was with Him constantly and closely observed His teaching and the miracles of His supreme goodness. One day, there appeared Joanna, a preeminent lady of substance (cf. Lk. 8:3). She heard the Lord preach that man who wished to be perfect should sell all his possessions and give to the poor, take up his cross and follow the Lord (cf. Mt. 19:21; 17:24). And so she renounced everything: she left her husband and her children her house and possessions and all her goods, followed the Lord and remained at all times close to His holy mother.

After that was the Feast of Tabernacles. Jesus, in addition to His miracles and healings, also did the following: He went into the temple with a whip and found there those who sold oxen, sheep, and turtle doves, as well as the money changers, and cast them out of the temple (cf. Mt. 21:12-13; Mk. 11:15-17; Lk. 19:45-46; Jn. 2:13-17). This was a manifest sign of the old and new Law. He put away the old Law and instituted the new. Then, after finishing His miracles in Judea, He returned to Galilee and travelled around to the cities and villages. He went to the city of Magdala, where Mary Magdalene followed Him (the Lord had cast seven demons out of her; cf. Lk. 8:2). She was renowned for her wealth and noble birth, and when she saw the Lord, she served Him zealously and faithfully, like His immaculate mother. Mary Magdalene was a pattern of our human nature, seized by seven evil spirits who oppose the seven gifts of the Holy Spirit: Human nature is plagued by seven chronic illnesses. So Mary Magdalene found the Physician and the Purifier of our nature, Him who mends every estrangement from God. And she was not only set free from all the demons by the grace of Christ but was also filled with this grace and demonstrated extraordinary zeal for the faith, mercy, and edifying thoughts. She followed the Lord for the rest of her earthly sojourn as His disciple and helper, she was the fair and obedient companion of the Queen, the holy Theotokos, and suffered together with her. And so she was found worthy in the end of the grace of an apostle. She travelled from place to place on Christ's behalf until she finally reached Rome, where she *fought the good fight* (1 Tim. 6:12) even *to the shedding of blood* (Heb. 12:4) for His sake and received the crown of martyrdom. And just as the blessed Peter was the most zealous of the Apostles, so also was Mary Magdalene the most zealous of the myrrh-bearers and the other women; but we shall discuss her good deeds in detail when we reach the chapter on Christ's crucifixion.

Now let us return to where we broke off our narrative and relate what happened next in the life of our Theotokos and Queen, her experiences with her Lord and Son and even those in connection with her own assumption. May my readers and listeners forgive me for this lengthy discourse, but this theme touches such great and profound mysteries that every tongue, every art, every faculty, every gift has always been, is always, and always will be employed, in all ages, from the first centuries until now, in the present world and the world to come.

Nevertheless, all this is and will always fall short of reality and pale in comparison, and no one, not even the noetic and incorporeal hosts of heaven, could ever express these divine and glorious mysteries adequately and fittingly, even should they describe and extoll them to the highest extent of their powers and arts.

So now let us return to our theme, as we said. After the supernatural and ineffable and immaculate birth, the incorruptible and most holy Mother was never separated from her blessed Son and King. He was her Lord even from childhood; she cared for Him as was fitting and ministered to Him as a servant. Wherever He went, she was always with Him. As I mentioned before, when Jesus had reached twelve years of age in the flesh, they went up to Jerusalem to celebrate the Passover, and when they went back, the child remained there. His spotless mother retraced her steps in distress and searched for Him frantically. When she found Him she asked Him dismayed: "Son, how could You do this to me?" And so on.

After that, Jesus returned with them and lived in Nazareth where He, the King and Lord of all, was obedient to them. And when He was thirty, He began His pastoral ministry, was baptized by John in the Jordan, where the Holy Spirit descended and remained upon Him in the form of a dove. There the Father bore witness from heaven that He was His beloved Son, and His holy mother followed Him always, wherever she could, and beheld His wonders and heard His preaching.

VI: ON THE PASSION

When the time came for the life-giving Passion, when our good, dearest Lord Jesus was judged by the chief priests and the rulers, tortured, and crucified, His immaculate mother was not only by His side the whole time but suffered with Him. And I would even venture to say, though it may sound bold, that she suffered even more than He, and her heart was filled with even more pain; for He was God and Lord of all things, and He willingly took the Passion upon His body (cf. Jn. 10:18). But she was subject to human and womanly frailty on the one hand, and was filled with perfect love for her dearly beloved and precious Son on the other; how could anyone express the flood of sorrow and tears when she saw the Passion of the dispassionate One, the greatest extreme of human pain? For once the divine and magnificent deeds of Christ had been done, the countless miracles, the divine teaching and preaching that He gave during His life on earth, there was nothing left undone but the consummation of the divine plan of salvation: the crucifixion, burial, and resurrection. There we see the suffering, pain, and sorrow of the holy Virgin, such that we cannot comprehend it with our mind or reason, for her love is inconceivable to us all. Indeed, when the time came for His Passion, it consumed all the others, like a fire that destroys everything in its path, when everyone forsook Him and fled, but it preserved His immaculate and grace-filled mother unscathed, like gold, refined and purified by the trial; for just as her glorious Son and God showed her to be a mother and a virgin at His birth, so also when the time came for His dispassionate Passion, He showed her compassion because of her motherly love, and even more because of the selfless affection that His most blessed mother bore towards Him; dispassionate love, by virtue of the divine grace that had saturated her soul; but also because of the supreme authority He had bestowed on His mother.

But let us return to where we began. We had said that she was inseparable from the Lord, her King and Son, and just as the Lord oversaw the twelve Apostles and then the seventy, so in a similar way His holy mother oversaw the other women who followed Him, as the holy Gospel says: *And many women who followed Jesus from Galilee, ministering to Him, were there* (Mt. 27:55). The holy Theotokos was their leader and caretaker. This is why during the Last Supper, when the Lord passed on to them the great mystery, He entrusted the care of those women who followed Him to His mother, that they might not fall into disarray, but also because He wished to honor and glorify her in this way. And indeed she comforted them and was a support in the toil of their souls and their ministry.

So the Lord Jesus was the head of the twelve Apostles and all the others who wished to be present, and passed on the supreme mysteries of the true and verily divine Passover, blessing them with His immaculate body and precious blood in the form of bread and wine, and revealed His inconceivable glory in utter humility, foreshadowing His Passion and resurrection. And thus He comforted and strengthened His disciples and revealed the true Passover to us all, preparing us at the same time to receive it with humility and the mind of a martyr. Jesus sat at the center of the table with His disciples and nourished their souls and bodies with the incorruptible food, having washed their feet with His hands. This was to teach them humility, give them strength to run the race of life, and make them rich with the adornment of truth, as it is written: *How beautiful are the feet of those who preach the gospel of peace* (Rom. 10:15; Is. 52:7).

But now the wicked one who shared His table betrays Him; the deceitful disciple steals from the blessed Lord. The feet just washed by the everlasting hands of his Maker now run to the Jews to barter for the priceless One. O who and what is he who could manifest such bestial thoughts of greed! *What are you willing to give me if I deliver Him to you?* said Judas Iscariot to the murderous chief priests; *And they counted out to him thirty pieces of silver. So from that time he sought opportunity to betray Him* (Mt. 26:15-16). And while the conniving disciple acted so treacherously, the merciful Lord and King of all things, according to the word of David (cf. Ps. 87:9), did not flee or try to escape, but was handed over, followed them, and *was led as a sheep to the slaughter* (Is. 53:7). He did not resist or protest but pressed on eagerly to the Passion. He was taken to the unworthy high priest, who in turn handed Him over to Pilate. They subjected Him to every kind of interrogation, but *as a lamb before the shearer is dumb, so He opens not His mouth. In His humiliation His judgment was taken away: who shall declare His generation?* (Is. 53:7-8). Pilate then announced the form of His martyrdom: crucifixion. This decision and decree was immediately relayed to His immaculate mother. Here you can see what this meant to her ineffable holiness and purity and even to her incomparable love for her Son, and how much pain she endured: For of all the disciples and the women, the friends and acquaintances who had followed Him to the Passion, some had deserted Him and fled in the face of His suffering, others had retreated to a distance, as it is written: *My friends and my neighbors* (cf. Mt. 26:31, 56; Ps. 36:12) have forsaken me; others followed Him at first, but then denied Him with an oath and finally *wept bitterly* (Mt. 26:75; Mk. 14:72; Lk. 22:62). But His true mother, glorious and blessed, who imitated Him exactly and so faithfully and closely intertwined herself with Him, not only because of their natural bond, but also because she had grown like Him by her virtues, and she displayed her magnificent power and wisdom, overshadowing all the wisdom and power not only of the other men and women around her, but of the entire human race, men and women of bygone generations and those yet to come. As in all other regards, so also during these most momentous events she proved to be the conqueror of all.

The only eternal virgin among women, though unused to the tumult of the crowd and the mob of vagabonds, armed soldiers, and officers, she nonetheless walked unafraid and never for a moment left the side of her dearly beloved Lord and Son, and clove to Him body and soul. She followed Him from the moment of her conception until the Passion had taken its course. She saw everything and heard His words. And so the sublime and most blessed Virgin could tell the disciples the greater part of the words the Lord had said during this time and the deeds He did both before and after His crucifixion. So when our Lord Jesus Christ stood before Annas and Caiaphas for questioning, the immaculate Virgin likewise followed Him and desired to go in with Him, but the wicked guards would not permit her. And so she anxiously questioned those who were coming in and going out what the charges against Him were, interrogating them closely to learn the truth. At the same time, she ascertained who was distressed at what was happening and who was pleased, for some of those who rightly discerning the gravity of the events informed her in secret; but the Virgin was able to see by herself those who were saddened and the others who were calloused and viciously accused Him, as well as those fools who not only spoke rationally, but yelled that He was not God but a lawbreaker, while it was *they* who were the scoffers and impure because of their ungodliness. They said, *Let us oppress the rightful Christ, for He is displeasing to us* (cf. Wis. 2:10-25).

Such were the things they concocted and contrived. But the blessed Virgin remained perfectly self-controlled in the face of all this, like an innocent dove amidst serpents and snakes, like a serene lamb amidst savage beasts, for she had completely devoted herself to the Passion of her Son and God, for it would bring victory in the end. Though she saw with her bodily eyes and heard with her ears the insults launched against Him, yet still her mind was totally fixed on Her dearest son, and she suffered likewise all that they inflicted on Him. She was heartbroken that the whole world had deserted Him and no one put up any resistance. Those who committed the injustice could not conceive that they were condemning to death the very Life of all.

What envy! The bottomless spring that gushes forth all evils; you taught us that first deadly rebellion and apostasy from God, and the second also, by leading Cain to murder his brother. And now you prevailed on the Jews to murder their God! Your evil venom ravages the whole world!

What a supreme mystery! The King of all things was counted among the prisoners, the intangible One was bound with chains, and His virgin mother remained by her Son and Lord Jesus to suffer and be crucified with Him of her own will. O mother of God, what anguish your heart suffered on your Son's behalf! O the tears that flowed from your eyes when you saw the Savior of all a prisoner, He who came to set the captives free with His hands bound behind His back like a brigand! The attendant savagely struck the One who is extolled and worshipped by the angelic hosts. Vile and wretched soldiers mocked and reviled Him. The godless unbelievers washed in their spittle that face by which we all receive the light. O His longsuffering! O His patience and inscrutable love for mankind! O blessed mother, what pain you had to endure!

And they stripped Him and put a scarlet robe on Him in mockery of Him who clothed His divinity in the nature of men. *When they had twisted a crown of thorns, they put it on His head* (Mt. 27:28, 29), the head of the King of all things, who put man in authority over all visible things. They paraded Him back and forth in jest, Him who causes the vault of heaven to tremble, they locked in a prison the One who *sets the sand as a bound for the sea* (Jer. 5:22) and *established the earth upon her sure foundation* (Ps. 103:5). The heart of His immaculate mother was like a storm-tossed sea, for just as her pregnancy had been supernatural, so also her love and anguish for Him were incomparable and inconceivable.

The great hour of surpassing sorrow came, and the cross was lifted up and borne by the King of angels. And the rebels crucified the

Creator of mankind and all else, the Lord and Maintainer of things visible and invisible. O how did the earth endure it and not collapse? How did the heavens not overturn when the evildoers hung Him on a tree who sits *enthroned upon the cherubim* (cf. Is. 37:16) and in the praise of the seraphim, who holds the heavens of the heavens in His hand! The vice-regent of the Father and the Holy Spirit endured the shame of crucifixion. He who *wraps Himself in light as a garment* (Ps. 103:2) was stripped naked and nailed to a cross! The murderers cast lots for the garment that His most holy mother had woven by hand and distributed amongst themselves the clothes of Him who was crucified. They drove nails through the hands that had created all things and held the heavens and the earth. O the goodness of the Lord! O His inexpressible patience! *Who shall tell the mighty acts of the Lord? Who shall cause all his praises to be heard?* (Ps. 105:2). But now, O mother of God, *a sword pierces through your own* heart, as Simeon had told you. Now the deep nails that the rebels drove through the hands of the Lord penetrate your heart. These woes distress you even more than your almighty Son, for He suffered of His own accord and had foretold all that He would undergo and desired it with all the force of His will. He had to lay down His life and His power and take it back up again, as the Gospel says (Jn. 10:17). But you suffered unbearable torment, for you did not know the full mystery of the Passion. And as the blood dripped from His incorruptible wounds, all this pain and sorrow tore through your heart and welled up springs of tears in your eyes. How could you have borne the sight of such a dreadful thing if the grace and power of your Lord and Son did not lend you strength and fortify you by His great mercy with the knowledge of His glory?

And in that hour, the merciful One even made supplication to the Father for the evildoers and asked Him to forgive them. O dearest King! The godless ones snapped at Him like dogs and handed Him over to jealousy and mockery, to blasphemy and ridicule. David of old had described their thoughts and deeds, speaking on the Lord's behalf: *They have opened their mouth against me, as a ravening and roaring lion* [...] *For many dogs have compassed me. The assembly of the evildoers has beset me round about. They pierced my hands and my feet. They counted all my bones* (Ps. 21:14, 17-18). Moreover, the Gospel confirms this: *And those who passed by blasphemed Him, wagging their heads and saying, "You who destroy the temple and build it in three days, save Yourself! If You are the Son of God, come down from the cross"* (Mt. 27:39-40). And the great David foreshadowed it: *The reproaches of them that reproached You have fallen upon me*, and also: *My soul has waited for reproach and misery; and I waited for one to grieve with me, but there was none; and for one to comfort me, but I found none.* There was none found to comfort Him. Now tell us, O prophet, what did they give you instead of comfort? *They gave me gall for my food and made me drink vinegar for my thirst* (Ps. 68:10, 21-22). Such was the comfort that they offered; this is how they repaid Him for all the good things they enjoyed. But when the most pure and blessed Mother of God saw and heard all these things, she felt the words of the mockers transfix her heart like arrows and the nails that held her Son. Then the earth trembled, Hades was broken, and the heavens were darkened, for their lights were put out and every creature mourned. The highest powers of the utmost heavens were shaken (cf. Mk. 13:25). Some of the celestial powers rocked the heavens in their shock, while others drew near to the place of the Skull (cf. Jn. 19:17) and stood aghast at the Jews' audacity. But all of them praised the King's patience and were incensed at the fallen angels and their wretched minions. They wished to fling the God-killers into the abyss and make Hades their grave (cf. Lk. 8:31). But the power and mercy of Christ curbed their desire and kept the impulse of all visible and invisible creation in check, that they might not be cast away utterly and *before the time* (cf. Mt. 8:29). For He had also called Moses to testify against the wickedness of the Jews: *Attend, O heaven, and I will speak; and let the earth hear the words out of my mouth* (Dt. 32:1), and what he goes on to proclaim. And He upbraided the Jews harshly with the words of Jeremiah: *The heaven is amazed at this, and is very exceedingly horror-struck, says the Lord* (Jer. 2:12), for they have forgotten His good deeds and repaid Him evil for good.

So then all creation was amazed and trembled, but the most holy mother of God wept more than any other creature, and nothing could console her. She felt her soul descend down into Hades, where affliction and sorrow reign, and all she desired was to draw near and hear a word from her blessed and humble Lord and Son. But she could not get close because of the throng surrounding her but had to stand far off and mourn. She lifted up her hands, beat her breast, and groaned from the depths of her heart. She herself was tortured by the Passion of her Son and watered the earth with her tears.

When the executioners had vented all their evil in His crucifixion, those who had contended with God dispersed. Some of them went to dine, while others returned to other activities, celebrating and amusing themselves as if they had achieved some victory, once they had set the soldiers to keep a close watch over Him. Then the Theotokos in her grief approached her dearly beloved Son. What tongue could describe what she said then or how she mourned before her crucified Son? Her words were choked by tears, but noble nonetheless, for she was the mother of Wisdom and could not give voice or expression to anything unbefitting, but remained within the bounds of decorum, grace, and serenity, though she had every right to grieve. She bitterly bewailed the suffering and the wounds of her dearest Lord and Son and praised His longsuffering and endurance, for He had suffered crucifixion for our sake, and she beheld Him in wonder. She rejected the thankless impudence of the God-slayers and mourned for their destruction. She said to the Lord:

"What is this, O Lord, my Son and my God? How exalted is Your patience? How could You, the sinless One, be counted among the godless? And even worse, be hung with the condemned, bearing the sins of the world, the Judge of the living and the dead! What a deep abyss of humility, patience, and love You display! Was it not enough that God became man on our behalf? Were the torments, threats, persecutions, plots, enmity, false witnesses, and slanderers that You have had to endure at the hands of the Jews since Your birth until now, when You would bring deliverance to men, were they not enough? But now, behold! They have nailed You to the tree! O what evil, what thanklessness and shamelessness on their part! And what unsurpassable mercy and longsuffering on Yours! The wicked Jews have tormented You in every way, You who smote Egypt of old for their sake! (cf. Ex. 7:14; 10:29).

"First they dressed You in a robe of mockery, You who once covered them in a brilliant cloud, led them like a Father, and kept them as the apple of Your eye! They placed on Your head a crown of thorns, You who *crowned them with glory and honor* (Ps. 8:6). They beat You with a staff, they for whom You commanded Moses to strike the sea with a staff. You split it in two and led them to the other shore, while the sea washed over their enemies. They in their jealousy dared to strike You, who have shown the light of Your face and given us life! You once glorified the face of Moses (Ex. 34:30), yet they did not shrink from spitting in Your face (O what unfathomable envy!);

You who opened by Your spittle the eyes of the man born blind (cf. Mk. 8:22-26). They drove nails through Your hands and feet, You who freed them of old from the chains of bondage in Egypt, and now from the ancient chains of bondage to the devil. To make the lepers clean, You were covered with wounds. To raise the dead to life, You were condemned to death. To give light to the eyes of the blind, O my Light! they did their utmost to close Your eyes. In exchange for You, O my Life! they asked for Barabbas and condemned You to death. O what a dreadful sight! How the earth can but tremble? Even the grave keeps its peace; how the stars fall dark and hide their light, how the heavens are shaken and yet they do not yet utterly fall, how the angels shudder and would overturn the universe if not checked by God's command! But this is clearly the work of Your compassion and patience, O my Son and my God, for all things submit to Your power; but You did not let the world be destroyed as in the days of Noah! Oh my Son! If only I could take Your place, if only I could suffer Your martyrdom! Alas! If only Your wounds could fall on me! Alas! If only I could receive death instead of You! It would not be so unbearable as Your death, for there can be nothing could bring me more pain than that. But I cannot die either in Your place or before You. I only ask that You grant me a word of comfort, dispose now of the remaining days of my life as You see fit. Count me worthy to hear the voice of Your greeting and Your proclamation that gladdens the world. When I meet You again, O my Light, I will embrace You, O my Life, and will hear Your dearest voice, by which You gave me life. And although You kept me from experiencing any throes or pangs at Your birth, now the sword of grief has pierced my heart as my eyes behold Your suffering. Now show me, I beseech You, Your glorious resurrection, as You so often promised me."

While the immaculate and blessed mother of God was thus mourning and sorrowing, the blessed Lord, rich in mercy, looked on her with affection; He saw the beloved disciple standing at her side, filled with love for his Lord and Teacher, and He who is Wisdom and Compassion itself, opened His mouth and had already prepared choice words for the occasion. He looked on the beloved disciple, he who had shown greater faith and love to His King and Lord than all the other disciples, as well as steadfastness and discernment of heart. For while all the others had fled, he alone remained by His side, rooted before the cross. So then Jesus spoke to His blessed mother: *Woman, behold your son!* and then to the disciple: *Behold your mother!* (Jn. 19:26-27). He gives to His virgin mother a likewise virgin son, and the disciple in His own place. For He could never fail to care for His immaculate mother! But He comforts His mother by offering her a visible consolation. For He Himself took invisible care of His mother and His disciple and of all that hope in Him, but He gave her to the disciple in exchange for the love and devotion he had shown by standing before Him in the hour of His suffering. And so He honored him immensely by leaving him in His place, and at the same time commanding us to care for and watch over our parents until the end, even if He in His foreknowledge did not always obey her fully. Indeed, He of whom Luke writes that He *was subject to them* before His baptism, after His baptism, in Cana of Galilee, He says to her: *Woman, what does your concern have to do with Me? My hour has not yet come* (Jn. 2:4). And when they say to Him: *Look, Your mother and Your brothers are standing outside, seeking to speak with You*, He answers: *Who is My mother and who are My brothers?* [...] *Here are My mother and My brothers!* (Mt. 12:47-49). While He used those words there as a compromise, now He clearly reveals all His affectionate care and love by leaving His disciple in His place, giving him to her as His substitute. He says to John: *Behold your mother!* He both comforts him in his bereavement and offers him His holy mother for his very own, as his charge and queen. When the disciple heard this, he took her home to the house of Zion (which we have already discussed in another chapter) and served her as befitted her by Christ's grace.

So once the godless executioners had had their fill of reviling and tyrannizing the blessed King, *Jesus, knowing that all things were now accomplished, that the Scripture might be fulfilled, said, "I thirst!"* (Jn. 19:28). And at once (as if they themselves thirsted for an even greater martyrdom), they offered *sour wine mingled with gall* (Mt. 27:34) (for shame!) to the sweet Nectar of life, the Spring of immortality. They revealed the utmost extremes of their evil, mingled with bitterness and inhumanity, that not one of the prophets' foretelling's might remain unfulfilled (cf. Ps. 68:22). But this did not happen because of the prophecy, but rather the prophecy revealed what would happen: for the prophecy did not cause their outrage, but the outrage of their disobedience had been the cause of the prophecy. So these envious and brutal men committed such audacities, forgetting the bitter waters of Marah (cf. Ex. 15:22-27; 17:1-7; Num. 20:11-13). But it was He who had made the waters fresh and so often given drink to the thirsty and cared for them in the arid wilderness with refreshing words: *They sucked honey out of the rock, and oil out of the solid rock* (Dt. 32:13). They had even forgotten the latter miracle of Cana in Galilee, where the water was turned into wine. Indeed, *their vine is of the vine of Sodom, and their vine-branch of Gomorrah: their grape is a grape of gall, their cluster is one of bitterness* (Dt. 32:32): this is the 'sour wine' and 'gall' that they always used to give their Benefactor to drink. But as for us, let us consider how His immaculate and most holy mother's heart was broken with crushing grief at the sight of all this; when she heard the words 'I thirst' from His sweetest and dearest mouth, what a fire flared up in her heart! At that moment her own heart was parched and scorched by the desire to quench her Son's last thirst, but the murderers would not let her bring Him even a drop of water. She begged every one of them to let her give Him some water to drink, but the beasts would not allow it. They did not let her comfort Him, but *opened their mouth against Him, as a ravening and roaring lion* (cf. Ps. 21:14). Instead of cool water, they gave Him gall and sour wine to drink. Before His crucifixion, *they gave Him wine mingled with myrrh to drink, but He did not take it* (Mk. 15:23), that He might not die an untimely and sudden death by the poison, and not of His own volition and free will. But when He was crucified, He took the sour wine mingled with bile, *He said, "It is finished!" And bowing His head, He gave up His spirit* (Jn. 19:30), voluntarily and by His own power.

But it is not in our power (or anyone else's) to depict the torments, the tears, and the heartbreak of the holy Virgin at the sight of her Son's suffering, for it surpassed human nature; and just as her pregnancy had been supernatural, so also the affliction she underwent at the Lord's crucifixion was beyond human conception. Only she who bore it can know, just as the Lord fully knew her from whom He was born. Finally, *Jesus cried out again with a loud voice, and yielded up His spirit* (Mt. 27:50). The Lord of all things Himself bows His head and summons death with a loud voice, who comes to Him as a slave, and thus the King completed His dispensation.

O blessed soul of the immaculate mother, stronger than steel! You are like a precious stone that stops the sword from piercing it altogether! How could the spotless Mother of God endure this agony? How could she herself not 'yield up her spirit'? It is clear that the grace of the crucified Lord protected her. He Himself yielded up His spirit as He saw fit, but His power preserved the soul of His mother in order to consummate her adornment by the pains she suffered and make her like Himself. Fear and trembling bind my tongue, and I cannot recount the events which followed, but the sharp arrows of Your sufferings drive me onward, Christ my King, and do not let me keep silent about this most precious story.

What other audacities did these foes and criminals commit, even after You had died? *The dregs* of their evil *have not been fully poured out* (cf. Ps. 74:9), not exhausted even by offering Him gall and sour wine, not even after He had yielded up His soul. No, the envy and frenzied aggression of these dread beasts and faithless God-killers was not curbed even by the anguish of His immaculate mother. Even if it had been animals they were torturing, they would have shown them some compassion. But they were harder and more calloused than stone, and even after He had died they pierced the life-giving side of Christ with a spear (cf. Jn. 19:34), lest they leave a single member of His body that did not suffer. His head endured the welts of the rod, His cheeks the blows, His mouth the bitter drink, and His face their spit before that; His back bore the lash, His hands and feet the nails, and now His side the spear, that from it might flow our salvation, the fountain of blood and water that makes us whole, and whereby He gave us the Holy Spirit (cf. 1 Jn. 5:6).

But you, O man, consider the sword which now pierced the heart of His blessed mother, and how she suffered all these things together with Him. And now she suffered even more, for she had almost reached the point of death at seeing her Son slain and anxious about His burial. And now on top of all these things, the sword that pierced His side also pierced her own heart. This wracked her with new pains, and the teardrops shone bright on the beautiful face of the virgin. The blood thickened in her heart, so that she could say, *My heart grew hot within me* and *my grief was renewed* (cf. Ps. 38:4, 3). So she ran up to Him and not only witnessed the twofold treasure with her own eyes, but received and inherited it as well; she reverently and boldly gathered the blood and water that flowed from the Life-giver's side, and so His loving and most blessed mother took the new and immortal spring of salvation as rich treasure for all.

She gave a sigh, as was only natural, but did not speak, not even then, but only words of lament. For now her only care was the burial of His life-giving body, for she could not bear it any longer to see Him hanging and broken like that, or endure even still the mocking and rancor of His foes. So she desired to find a fitting sanctuary, but could not find any place that was worthy, that could meet the requirements for receiving the life-giving body of her Son, as her immaculate womb had been found worthy to receive the fullness of the Godhead. She was not looking for anything more than a place equal to her desire and zeal. This is why she scoured all of the Place of the Skull, driven by the grace of His dead, yet life-giving body. Her limbs moved about, but her eyes and mind were fixed on the love of her King and Son. So, led by the grace, she found a beautiful grave, a little ways away from the cross, and all about it a lovely garden. The grave was empty, freshly hewn out of the living stone: a new grave, in which (as the holy Gospel informs us) *no one had yet been laid.* It was awaiting the newly-slain sacrifice, the Lord and God of all. By divine providence, it was completely unused, because of the impending resurrection, that no one might claim that someone else's body had come back to life and not Christ's. This is why no one had been laid there, as the Gospel says: *Now in the place where He was crucified there was a garden, and in the garden a new tomb in which no one had yet been laid* (Jn. 19:41). It was new, for it would house the *new Adam* (cf. Rom. 5:14); and since it had never received anyone yet, it was irreproachable of any treachery or human failing, and would let no one take refuge in false testimony or graverobbing. So it was, in every way, above suspicion. The rock was hewn out for the *Cornerstone* (cf. Ps. 117:22; Eph. 2:20), a triumphal arch for the *Incorrupt One* (cf. Ps. 15:10; Acts 2:31), a bedrock for the unshakeable *Foundation* (cf. 1 Cor. 3:11). This place of the Skull was a pattern of the Garden of Eden, for here Adam was buried. The Passion that He brought to pass here set us free from our passions, just as the death of the deathless One put an end to death.

When the most holy Mother of God saw this nearby spot, a grave so suitable and beautiful and unused, that should protect His body from decay, she inquired after it and learned that it belonged to a certain Joseph, who was also himself *a disciple of Jesus, but secretly, for fear of the Jews* (Jn. 19:38). So she explained to him with a single word that she was truly the mother of the Word and the mother of Wisdom. She not only asked him for the grave, for she knew that this would be easy and agreeable to him: that is, to give his grave to his good and blessed Shepherd and Teacher, keep Him there like buried treasure. But rather she prevailed on him to take Jesus down from the cross himself and keep watch over him, for this was difficult and required great courage. Moreover, Joseph was a wealthy and honorable man, and known to Pilate. The most holy Mother of God called to him and said: "My good friend, look what has come of the hatred and madness of the foes and priestly judges of the Lord our God, my Son Jesus Christ. They put Him to death, most bitterly and unjustly, and rained down blows and mockery on Him both before and after His crucifixion; and now His naked body hangs on a tree! A dread sight to me and to every creature. After His death they pierced His side with a spear, and out flowed blood and water (what a miracle!), yet still the God-slayers did not revere even this. The sun was darkened, the earth shook, the rocks split, the curtain of the temple tore in two, and yet they remained unfeeling and hard-hearted. They reviled and mocked Him. They wagged their heads at Him in jest. But as for you, demonstrate now your reverence for God in deeds, your love and trust in your Teacher and King. Be the consolation for my sorrow and mourning over Him. Go to Pilate and ask for His body which hangs on the cross, and offer on your own initiative your own grave. Pluck up the courage to lay to rest there the treasure of the whole world. By God's help you will buy and obtain the salvation of all who live. Offer to your Teacher this service, and you will receive grace at the consummation of His dispensation. Now stand firmer than the other disciples and keep your wits about you, for some of them forsook Him utterly, while others retreated in the face of His Passion. I alone, of no account and foreign, together with a single disciple, I remained and mourned among those beasts. I am too frail and poor, rich and powerful only in tears and pain. I do not require consolation from anyone. Behold, my King and my Son, He Himself will run to meet you in this service, the dead One who raises the dead, He who rocked the foundations of the earth, put out the sun and shook all of creation."

And so the most wise and blessed of women encouraged Joseph and sent Him to Pilate. He went to Pilate and with the Lord's courage and cunning, he asked for the body of Christ. He did not fear his power nor the wrath of the Jews. And so he received his heart's desire. He asked and received in exchange for his words the Word of God; in exchange for his garden, he purchased the heavens; in exchange for his grave, life; in exchange for seeking the Teacher, boldness before the King of all. Indeed, Joseph was not only rich but wise, even wiser than the *merchant*, who, as the holy Gospel says, *when he had found one pearl of great price, went and sold all that he had and bought it* (Mt. 13:46). But Joseph did not only give 'all that he had', but all his desire, great courage, his rock and his grave in order to buy the 'pearl of great price' which he kept in unfading remembrance. This disciple of Jesus was the exact opposite of Judas. While Judas had plotted and schemed to betray his merciful Teacher and Lord to His enemies, Joseph himself now delivers himself to those enemies to ask for the body of his Lord and Teacher. Judas turned Him over to His murderers for a handful of money, while Joseph made obeisance and offered his fortune to ask the murderers to return Him to Joseph's reverent keeping. Judas delivered Him over to by crucified by a treacherous kiss, while Joseph took Him down from the tree and embraced Him warmly, clothed Him richly in love, and honored Him by sharing in His suffering. The traitorous disciple led the evil band of Jews to Him with swords and torches and delivered over to them the merciful Lord. Joseph took Him down from the tree, pulled out the nails, and returned the dearest life-giving gift to His mother, without peer in all of creation.

His blessed mother shared in Joseph's suffering as they took her King and Son down from the cross. She watered the earth with her tears and received His divine body into her arms, taking the nails into her lap, and lovingly embraced His wounded limbs; she washed the blood away with her tears, bitterly bewailing the dearest Bridegroom of angels and men. And once that body, exalted above the heavens, had been taken down from the cross and laid out on the ground, she showered it with her hot tears, crushed and broken-hearted, and composed the divine words of the burial lamentation:

"O the consummation of the awful mystery! O the revelation of the hidden counsels of eternity past (cf. Eph. 1:7-12)! O the death, more wondrous even than the incarnation! Lifeless lies the Maker of life; He who gives salvation to all now rests in death; the Word of the Father speaks no more; He who created all that has speech and voice; closed and motionless are now the eyes of Him who set in motion all that moves, by a single word, by a single nod; He who makes the mountains melt at the sight of Him (Ps. 96:5), for He is the One *who looks upon the earth, and makes it tremble; who touches the mountains, and they smoke* (Ps. 103:32). This dead man sees the thoughts of all men and *searches the hearts and thoughts* (Ps. 7:10); He gives light and understanding to the blind, and yet the sons of men still insist on evidences! Alas! Where is Your beauty now, O my Son and my God? Where is Your comely form, *more beautiful than the sons of men* (cf. Ps. 44:3)? Every good thing on earth came from You, for you are the dearest desire of all things. You took the blows and the wounds, You who healed the incurable disease of our nature, the sores, all our wounds, both old and new. Thus were you scourged for our sake, O Lord, by Your great mercy, and *by Your bruises we are healed* (cf. Is. 53:5; 1 Pet. 2:24). And behold, through Your long-suffering and love for all men, the mystery of Your design was brought to pass by Your grace. And now show Your power! Come swiftly to our aid! I surely know that You will rise again and have mercy first on Your mother and then on Zion and all of Jerusalem, which has sinned so grievously against You; You will summon all the nations to her (cf. Mic. 4:1-2) and will constitute the temple out of the living Church of the nations. O how blessed will be that day in which You grant me to hear again Your dearest voice. Then I will bask in the divine beauty of Your face and be filled with Your grace, which I desire with all my heart. I will be blessed when I see You clearly as the true God and Lord of the living and the dead."

Now how could I, unworthy and untrained, give fitting voice to and describe the words that the holy Mother of God uttered in those moments? Even if all the tongues of the wise and learned were gathered together, even they could not do it justice; but I only render the barest outline of her words, in order to fulfill the expectations of the godly.

With these words and in this frame of mind, the Mother of God wept bitterly and took the incorrupt and life-giving body of the Lord Jesus into her spotless hands, together with Joseph and Nicodemus. When they had anointed Him with myrrh and wrapped Him in *a clean linen cloth* with aloes *and laid it in his new tomb which he had hewn out of the rock; and he rolled a large stone against the door of the tomb* (Mt. 27:59-60; Lk. 23:53). And when Joseph and Nicodemus had discharged their service with all propriety, they left the grave in the company of some others who were with them. But the holy and immaculate mother of the Lord remained there alone and watched with unwearying eyes of the soul and the body. She knelt down and prayed unceasingly and without pause, eagerly asking when the sweet light of the resurrection would dawn.

Now there stood by the cross of Jesus His mother, and His mother's sister, Mary the wife of Cleopas, and Mary Magdalene (Jn. 19:25). We have already spoken about Mary Magdalene in order to comment on a common question. As the other three Gospels say: *And many women who followed Jesus from Galilee, ministering to Him, were there looking on from afar* (Mt. 27:55). The glorious Gospel writer John the Theologian, however, recounts how His mother and the other two Mary's (the wife of Cleopas and Mary Magdalene) were standing near Jesus. And as we know, both of these accounts are true and took place as they are recorded. There were many women who followed Jesus from Galilee and ministered to Him, among others these two Mary's. But the men's courage utterly failed, as did their fortitude and bravery, and their sublime thoughts that were supposed to so transcend the rest of the rabble. This is why some of the Gospel writers do not record the names, for they could not have known who was there. But John records the names and even informs us of the relations between them: Mary the wife of Cleopas, the sister of Jesus' mother, and Mary Magdalene. Mary the wife of Cleopas was married to the brother of Joseph, who had been betrothed to the Virgin Mary, for Cleopas was Joseph's brother. John further refers to Mary, the holy Mother of God, by her mother's family, and this is why he calls her 'His mother's sister', for she was the sister of Jesus' mother. But Matthew writes as follows: *Many women who followed Jesus from Galilee, ministering to Him, were there looking on from afar, among whom were Mary Magdalene, Mary the mother of James and Joses, and the mother of Zebedee's sons* (Mt. 27:55-56). Mark likewise mentions them by name (cf. Mk. 15:40). Luke does not mention the names, but says: *But all His acquaintances, and the women who followed Him from Galilee, stood at a distance, watching these things* (Lk. 23:49). For when the Lord's passion was upon Him, certain women followed Him from afar, and when He was crucified, they stood a ways off and watched from there. But the two Mary's loved the Lord more fervently than they and participated in the agony and the pangs of His immaculate mother. And so they looked on fearlessly and with lofty thoughts from under the cross of the Virgin's Son. But those who hung back also showed sterner mettle, for they left the crowd and came a little closer, comforting her and suffering with her. This is why the Gospel says: *there stood by the cross of Jesus His mother, and His mother's sister, Mary the wife of Cleopas, and Mary Magdalene* (Jn. 19:25). But even though they were stronger than the other women, they could not match the fortitude of the Mother of God's soul. This is why, when the commotion of the Jews had subsided somewhat, they plucked up their courage and came near to the place where the immaculate and most holy Virgin now stood, at the foot of the Lord's cross. But when the Lord threw the Godopposers into an uproar by signaling that He was thirsty, and they began preparing the mixture of sour wine and gall, the women lost their nerve and fled. But the most blessed stood fast by her crucified Son, unafraid. When they brought Him down from the cross, however, and took Him to the grave, the women did not dare to approach, but were *sitting opposite the tomb* (cf. Mt. 27:61), which means that they were sitting a long ways off and watching (cf. Lk. 23:55), as the Gospels say. And when the chief priests and the scribes came with the soldiers to set watchmen over the grave to guard it, and to seal it with a stone and secure it, the women were terrified and ran away. They were torn between fear of the Jews on the one hand and love for Christ on the other. They departed and went to buy spices (cf. Lk. 23:56). And early on the morning of the first day after the Sabbath, they returned to see the tomb and anoint the holy body of the Lord (cf. Lk. 27:1). If they had not left, how could they have prepared the spices? So it is clear that this is why they departed and came back with the spices: to give a practical display of worship and faith.

VII: AT THE RESURRECTION

Now, the immaculate Mother of God had not moved from the tomb in the slightest. She observed all that happened and heard all that was said. She saw the mighty earthquake that woke the departed saints from their slumber (cf. Mt. 27:51-53; 1 Cor. 15:20), while at the same time putting the guards to sleep (cf. Mt. 28:4, 13) and moving the stone; she also saw how the guards later awoke and went into the city (cf. Mt. 28:11). The women who had left and returned later could not have witnessed any of this, but the blessed Mother of God, spellbound by her love for her Son and rooted immovably by the tomb, beheld with her own eyes all these things, even unto His glorious resurrection. While the other women did find the stone rolled away and the angel sitting on it (cf. Mt. 28:4), they had no way of knowing when or how this had happened. Only the immaculate Mother of the Lord, who had not moved from her place, knew the whole story. This is why she received news of the resurrection before the others and was found worthy to see this awesome sight before anyone else: her Lord and God arisen, the greatest good we could conceivably desire. She heard His sweetest voice and believed in what she had seen of the mysteries of His design. Just as she had once believed in His incarnation, so now she also believed in His resurrection. Not only because she was His immaculate and holy mother, but also because she had remained by His side throughout his passion and suffered bitterly with Him, drawing what strength her soul needed from Him, that she might not die with Him. And so, the most holy Mother of the Lord beheld first of all the resurrection of her Son. She relayed this to His disciples and was the first to announce it to the myrrh-bearers. Even if the Gospel writers do not mention anything about this per se, it is a certainty due to her close affinity with Him. They refrained from recounting His mother's testimony because she had already been convinced beforehand, and someone might use that as a pretense for disbelief if His mother were to describe how she saw Christ's resurrection. And moreover, some would claim that the Gospels do not record this out of deference for the holy Queen and for her testimony. This is why they do not mention this fact anywhere, but rather describe the accounts of the other myrrh-bearers.

So the holy Mother of God saw with her own eyes the resurrection of her Son and King, and returned overjoyed from the grave and went to the house of the Beloved Disciple, where she awaited the hour of Christ's assumption. This house was built on Zion, as I said before. John the Evangelist had sold his family estate in Galilee after the death of his father Zebedee and bought this house in Zion in Jerusalem, where he now brought the Mother of God to live, just as his Lord and Teacher had commanded him, and ministered to her there. Buying this house had put him on familiar terms with the chief priest, as the Gospel says: *that disciple was known to the high priest* (Jn. 18:15). This was where the other disciples *were assembled, for fear of the Jews*. And this is where the Lord appeared after His resurrection, *when the doors were shut*, and *He breathed on them and said to them, "Receive the Holy Spirit"* (cf. Jn. 20:19, 22). It was also there, eight days later, that He fulfilled Thomas' request and showed them *the print of the nails* (cf. Jn. 20:27). There the Apostles, after the Lord had been taken up, performed the first divine liturgies, and that house was the abode of the Mother of God during all that time. And His holy and most glorious mother dwelled in that very house both before and after His assumption (cf. Acts. 1:13-14), awaiting His ascent to heaven, for that would signal the completion of His purpose and His entire earthly life. And so from the resurrection until the assumption, the Lord appeared many times to His most holy mother, as He saw fit, and more than once He comforted her in accordance with His good pleasure. He did not appear to the disciples anymore except when necessary, and He also ate repeatedly in their presence (cf. Lk. 24:43, Jn. 21:12, 14), that they might believe that He was not appearing to them as a vision but as the true Lord Jesus Christ, their King and Teacher. So when He had *opened their mind* (Lk. 24:45) to understand many of His mysteries, He promised to send them the Holy Spirit after Him and commanded them to *tarry in the city of Jerusalem until you are endued with power from on high. And He led them out as far as Bethany, and He lifted up His hands and blessed them* (Lk. 24:49-50). The holy Mother of God was also present, for she could not miss such a great moment. And just as her heart was more broken than any other during His passion, yet she still remained by His side, so she also desired to see His glorious assumption. And she certainly did see it and was filled with joy.

Now the Lord, as I said, blessed the Apostles and promised them the Holy Spirit. But His immaculate and holy mother He had blessed from the beginning, from when she had first heard the words, *Rejoice, highly favored one, the Lord is with you; blessed are you among women!* (Lk. 1:28). She received this fountain of blessing into her womb and brought into the world the Breaker of the ancient curse. And so she had been filled with the Holy Spirit since the beginning, and had already been *clothed with power from on high* (Lk. 24:49). This happened the day the Archangel Gabriel said to her, *The Holy Spirit will come upon you, and the power of the Highest will overshadow you* (Lk. 1:35). And so every promise had been fulfilled in her, and she had been crowned Queen of heaven and earth, just as her Son had received *all authority in heaven and on earth* (Mt. 28:18) when He rose from the dead, not only as God but also as man.

So when the Lord was taken up and the Apostles and His most holy mother saw Him ascend into heaven, He immediately sent angels to encourage them (cf. Acts 1:10-11) and to announce to them His impending second coming. And they worshipped Him and returned to Jerusalem filled with great joy (Lk. 1:28; 24:52). *These all continued with one accord in prayer and supplication, with the women and Mary the mother of Jesus, and with His brothers* (Acts 1:14); and the holy Mother of God was a constant paragon and guide in all virtue.

After Christ's assumption, she remained in her house and became the true source of every virtue and the treasury of all good things. Just as she used to live in her sanctuary and was an example and a guide to all virtue, so also after the assumption the holy Mother of God was a role model both for the men and for the women, leading them in every good work by the grace and aid of her glorious Son and King. This is why she exhorted the Apostles to keep a tighter regimen of fasting and prayer. And so they devoted themselves to fasting, prayer, and petition, until the day of Pentecost arrived and they were filled with the grace of the Holy Spirit, the Comforter of souls. From then on, the venerable Apostles went out preaching the gospel and spreading the word of life throughout Jerusalem and all of Judea, and ultimately to the ends of the earth, as the Holy Spirit instructed, making *disciples of all the nations, baptizing them in the name of the Father and of the Son and of the Holy Spirit* (Mt. 28:19), according to the Lord's commandment.

Meanwhile, the Lord's mother remained in the house of the Beloved Disciple in Zion, and lived out the remaining holy days of her godly life in accordance with her unspeakable glory and grandeur, for the rest of her life was even more surpassingly miraculous and supernatural! I would say that, with the exception of the awesome and ineffable conception and childbirth (for the mysteries of the divine birth surely surpassed all nature and created order), she was even more exalted and wondrous than before. I mean her contemplative activity and holy conduct, for her latter works were not in the slightest inferior to the former. Indeed, consider that if she had not been born and bred by a miracle herself, then how could she have conceived and raised the Son and Word of God, the King and God of all, such an indescribable and inscrutable marvel? So she continued to work marvelous miracles all the days of her life, winning impossible victories over nature by her innate strength of will, and utterly vanquishing the spiritual enemy of mankind. And once her labors were complete, after she had shared in the sufferings of the Lord and borne so many hardships, trials, afflictions, sorrows at the cross, she was crowned the conquering victor with many crowns and the Queen over all creation. And then, greatest of all, she beheld her Son – the Son and Word of the Father, the true God and King of all – rise from the grave and ascend into heaven clothed in the nature she had given Him.

After all this glory, her life was truly free of labor and toil. This does not, of course, mean that the immaculate Virgin lacked physical struggles and contemplative ascents, but once she began her divine life of inner contemplation that was a blessing to all, she did not *give sleep to her eyes, nor slumber to her eyelids, nor rest to her temples* (cf. Ps. 131:4), nor respite to her body; while the Apostles were scattered throughout all the world, the holy Mother of God and Queen of all dwelt in the center of the world, Jerusalem, on holy Zion, together with the Beloved Disciple whom the Lord Jesus Christ had given her as a son.

And while she sent out the Apostles to preach to *those who were afar off and those who were near* (Eph. 2:17), she herself remained in the royal city of Zion, for she had become the target of aggression and hardships on account of her Son. On His behalf she confronted and struggled against His enemies, the wicked Jews, and at the same time she acted as mediator and ambassador of all, not only the believers, but also showing mercy even to the unbelievers. And so she led them to knowledge and repentance, for so she had been taught by her blessed Son as he hung on the cross, saying: *Father, forgive them, for they know not what they do* (Lk. 23:34). And moreover, she herself was also filled with divine grace and long-suffering, *desiring all men to be saved and come to the knowledge of the truth* (1 Tim. 2:4).

And she did not stop there but added labor upon labor of fasting and prayer. She was almost inseparable from the Lord's grave, dwelling there at the place where she had laid her head. The stone was her pillow, her contemplative occupation was supplications to her Son, her diet was heartfelt jubilation, her food was telling, recounting, and recalling the sufferings of the Lord, her drink and ablutions were tears, her rest and delight were her prostrations. Indeed, faithful witnesses have claimed, and the report has reached our ears that her most holy hands calloused over from all her prostrations; those very hands with which she had once cradled the Lord, born from her without seed of man. But now again she lifted them to heaven and entreated and besought Him without ceasing. But who could fully describe her godly works, which would be far too long to recount one by one? But what all have noticed and agree on is that she as the successor of her King and Son became an example by His grace, the guide and queen of the faithful who hope in His name, men and women alike, His companions and disciples. This is why she was the center of everyone's care and struggle, and all eyes looked to her in trust. Now they saw her who had carried the Lord Jesus Christ bodily into the world, His most holy and blessed mother, in the place that He had occupied when He dwelt in the flesh among men. This was a comfort and an encouragement to them in their discipline of the body, patient endurance in trials, and forbearance toward all.

But His immaculate mother was more than just an encouragement and a living instruction in patience and endurance for the blessed Apostles and the other Christians, but she also took part in their efforts, strengthened them in their preaching, and participated in their poverty, their afflictions, and their imprisonment. She bore hardship with them, just as she had shared in the Lord's suffering in the pangs of her heart. Moreover she now gave the holy disciples just as much comfort by her good deeds as by her words, setting the suffering of her King and Son as an example for them. She reminded them of the rewards and the crowns of the kingdom of heaven, and the eternal bliss and gladness. So when Herod arrested Peter, the chief Apostle, bound him in chains (cf. Acts 12:6-7), and threw him in prison, she also, the holy and blessed Mother of God, was there with him in spirit, *had compassion on him in his chains* (cf. Heb. 10:34), and interceded for him, urging the Church to pray as well. And before, when the wicked Jews had stoned Stephen (Acts 7:59), and Herod executed James the brother of John (Acts 12:2), the pain of the sword pierced the heart of the holy Mother of God, and she was made a martyr together with him by the pangs of her heart and her many tears.

We have also been told by our Fathers that when the Apostles scattered to preach the gospel, each to the land he had been appointed, the holy John the Theologian and Evangelist remained there to serve and care for the holy Mother of God whose son he had become, according to the Lord's commandment. The holy Queen then said to him, by the grace of Christ: "It does not seem right to me, my son, that your friends and brothers are going to preach in the name of Christ my Son and my God, and win disciples among the nations, while you remain here doing nothing in order to care for me. And yet I am loath to part with you without the Lord's consent, for He has commanded us to be together. So now go to the land you have been appointed to, and I will follow, that we may fulfill both: that you may preach, and I may remain always at your side." This was her suggestion to the Beloved Disciple, and she left to accompany him in his preaching, taking Mary Magdalene and the other myrrh-bearers.

Then her merciful Lord and Son appeared to her in a vision and instructed her to return home. He commanded that the Beloved Disciple continue on his way, and that the myrrh-bearers accompany him to encourage and assist him. So He commanded them at first to set off together with him, that the zeal and willingness of the holy Queen might be apparent, and because the Evangelist did not wish to leave the most holy Mother of God; and she was of the same mind. But then, by instructing her to return, He honored her even more highly by distinguishing her from the Apostles, but at the same time uniting her even more closely with them, for in this way they could visit her even more easily. The Mother of God could also lead the faithful people and the church of Jerusalem, working in tandem with James, who had been installed there as bishop. In fact, every place she went, she blessed by her presence. So she returned to Jerusalem and remained there in the house of John as she had before. But the Theologian and Evangelist made for Ephesus in the province of Asia, according to the Lord's commandment. With him went the myrrh-bearers and Prochorus, one of the seven deacons (cf. Acts 6:5). There he preached the name of Jesus as God and gave light to those who were in darkness; the august myrrh-bearers shared in his struggles and became apostles themselves. Some died there by persecution, shedding their blood as martyrs and departing with their crowns to be with their Lord and Teacher Jesus Christ.

Meanwhile, after John the Evangelist had departed, James the blessed, the brother of Joseph, called the Brother of God, served and waited on the Mother of God, considering this ministry to be the utmost blessing. He became the first bishop of Jerusalem and cared for and served the holy Mother of God in John the Evangelist's stead. And so the return of the Mother of God to Jerusalem was truly a blessing, for in this way it became the refuge, the safe haven and the support of the infant Church. The Christians trusted the immaculate Virgin in every challenge and trial. According to the Jews, they were often the most unruly firebrands among the people and constantly found themselves facing adversities and death because of their faith in Christ; these they endured willingly. It was the Virgin, though, that consoled and refreshed them.

And so she was a source of blessing and hope for both the first generation of Christians and those to follow, and is and will continue to be the intercessor and strong help until the end of the world. But in those days her struggle was all the more difficult, since the new gospel way of life had to be modelled perfectly and instituted, to the glory of Christ's name. And all the attacks launched against the Church, the outrages committed against the believers' homes and persons, many of whom lost their lives, were thrown into prison, and suffered abuse of every sort, persecutions, enslavement, including the afflictions of the Apostles who were driven from place to place – all of these were echoed by her. She suffered for each one of them individually and cared for them all in word and deed. She was the paragon of every virtue and spurred them on to even greater things, to the place of her Lord and Son, as the mediator and intercessor to Him on behalf of all the faithful. She implored Him to cover all the believers with His mercy and protection. And to the holy Apostles she was a guide and teacher, and they referred every problem that arose to her. They consulted her and received her exhortations to virtue, and those who lived near Jerusalem went regularly to visit her at Zion. They saw her often and told her of their work and their preaching, and they followed all of her instructions. But even those who lived far away returned eagerly once a year to Jerusalem at Easter to celebrate Christ's resurrection with the Mother of God. Each of them recounted to her the story of his preaching among the nations and the persecutions he suffered at the hands of both Jews and gentiles. And then they returned to continue their mission, strengthened by her prayers and admonitions.

Barring serious impediments, all of them did this every year, with the single exception of Thomas. He could not come because of the great distance and hardships of journeying from India. But all the others came yearly to visit the holy Queen, and afterward returned to the work of spreading the gospel, encouraged by the strength of her prayers.

But who could enumerate the attacks and plots of the wicked Jews, the uproar and hostility of the unbelievers? Who could describe the slander, the ridicule, the doubt cast on the Lord's miracles, and the false testimony against Christ's resurrection? For they claimed that the disciples had stolen His body, as the holy Gospel records: *this saying is commonly reported among the Jews until this day* (Mt. 28:15). They would often gather in hopes of stoning the house where the Mother of God dwelt, but the power of Christ frustrated their plans. Once, however, the children of wrath (cf. Eph. 2:3) formed a murderous band, the wicked offspring, *a forward and perverse generation, a foolish people and unwise, a nation that has lost its counsel, and there is no knowledge in them* (Deut. 32:5-6, 28). Their wrath is like the venom of asps, that stubbornly shuts its ears that it may not hear (cf. Ps. 57:5-6).

These wicked God-slayers plotted to set fire to the house wherein dwelt the treasure of life, the mother of the Lord Jesus Christ, and they would have truly razed it to the ground. They went with burning torches in their hands, stones, and iron spades. They surrounded the city of God with shouts, but they could not even approach it, for the holy city was even stronger than they, as the Prophet had said: *Wondrous things are said of you, O city of God* (Ps. 86:3). In fact, their own fire turned against them and burned many of the evildoers. The stones they cast at the roof of the holy house turned back on them and crushed many. Their bars and spades were bent and broken, and their evil plan was thwarted. *Their trouble shall return on their own head, and their unrighteousness shall come down on their own crown* (cf. Ps. 7:17). Their own sword pierced their hearts and their bows were splintered; and many were plunged living into Hades (cf. Deut. 32:32).

When all the believers saw what had happened, they praised Christ: *The righteous shall rejoice when he sees vindication* (Ps. 57:10), says the Prophet. Such were the plots and schemes of the envious Jews who never ceased from their heinous ways from the most ancient times up until the present, when they even went so far as to condemn to death the most blessed King and Creator of all things, *even the death of the cross* (cf. Phil. 2:8). And now again, as if that were not enough for them, those impudent rogues vented their hostility on His immaculate mother. But their trouble returned on their own head (cf. Ps. 7:16). And even after so many great wonders their hard hearts did not change, but even at the hour of her death they displayed one last time their vile and frenzied hatred for God, as we shall see when we come to that point.

But now let us return and continue our story. Once these wonders had taken place and the foes of Christ and His most holy Mother were punished, those sinners did not have the courage to attempt another such outrage. The holy Virgin and Mother of God did not encounter any more distain on their part, but they viewed her with reverence and kept their distance. They respected and feared her, forgetting their unbounded fury, which had become habitual for them, like it is for dogs. This was not only a result of those miracles in particular and the just retribution their attack had received, but also because of the daily miracles she worked by her grace and intercession. Demons were cast out, incurable diseases were healed, and countless signs and wonders were wrought by her hand. In addition to all this, a light and radiance shone forth from her face, which gave grace to the believers and struck fear into the foes; for Christ, the King of all and her Son, had glorified His immaculate and holy Mother by making her dwelling place impenetrable to all those who opposed and plotted against her. And by the grace and the mediation of the most holy Mother of God, the faithful people grew and became numerous, and the faith of the Christians was strengthened.

Moreover, our Lord Jesus Christ so willed that His most holy mother should live in the world for many more years, so that the believers would be encouraged all the more by her grace, and the Church would flourish, to the glory of the Father and the Son and the Holy Spirit. And so, the most blessed and glorious Mother of God, having found such favor with her Son, lived to a great age. The Queen of all creation almost reached eighty years of this fleeting life and did not cease her labors, praying and beseeching her Son. On the contrary, day by day she advanced toward perfection in every good work. She always appeared simple and unassuming, but her majesty manifested itself in the great heroism that she displayed. As we have been told by reliable witnesses, she even hollowed out grooves in the marble floor of the holy house of Zion by her pious prostrations, as well as in the stone pillow she used when her bodily nature forced her to take a little sleep. Moreover she lived in abject poverty, by necessity of her compassion. The gilded and precious objects she was given were put to good and surprising use, so that her riches were turned into penury, and her generosity into privation, because of her simple heart. She did not only have compassion on her friends and acquaintances, but also on strangers and even enemies, for she was the mother of compassion, the mother of the only compassionate and loving One, who *makes His sun to rise on the evil and the good and sends rain on the just and the unjust* (Mt. 5:45). She was the mother of Him who took on flesh and died on a cross for us while we were sinners and renegades, in order that He might pour out His mercy over us. Truly she gave birth to poverty and indigence, but also to riches, for the rich One became poor for our sake, that He might make us poor wretches rich.

Up until this point, we have touched briefly on her labors, compassion and the general greatness of her virtues. So now to sum up what we have said: She gave birth supernaturally to the incarnate Son and Word of God, she lived with otherworldly conduct and was proclaimed victor over all generations who had gone before and would come after by virtue of her generosity, the height and depth of her virtues and her good works. She was magnified and so exceeded all others as the sun outshines the stars.

VIII: THE DORMITION

Now, by her grace, we shall speak of her departure and translation from the present world into the eternal kingdom of her Son. For the tale is truly resplendent and joyous to hear for those who love God.

So when Christ our God saw fit to translate His most holy and immaculate mother from this world into His kingdom, that she might receive the imperishable crown for her supernatural struggles and virtues, and to place her *at His right hand, clothed in vesture wrought with gold, and arrayed in many colors* (cf. Ps. 44:12), as befits the Mother of God, and to proclaim her Queen over all creation, leading her behind the curtain and seating her in the heavenly Holy of Holies; and so he intimated to her beforehand her own glorious rapture. He sent the archangel Gabriel to her again to announce her magnificent departure, just as He had announced her wondrous conception. So the archangel visited her and gave her a palm branch, a symbol of victory, which the people had used to welcome her Son into Jerusalem as the conqueror of death and the destroyer of Hades (cf. Mt. 21:1-11). So now also Gabriel gave this bough to the Virgin as a symbol of the victory over the terrors and dissolution of death, saying: "Your Lord and Son is calling you: 'The time has come for you to come to Me, O my good mother' (cf. Song 2:10, 13). For this reason He has sent me again to you, O *blessed among women*, for today you will delight the heavenly hosts with your ascent, O *highly favored one*, and will shine brighter than the souls of the saints, just as you filled those on earth with gladness. So now you yourself rejoice together with them, just as you gave them joy; for from now on *all generations* (cf. Lk. 1:48) of reasonable creatures *will call you blessed* for all eternity. *Greetings, highly favored one, the Lord is with you.* Your prayers and petitions have gone up to heaven to your Son, and so according to your request He has instructed for you to leave this world and ascend into the heavenly dwellings, that you might be with Him always, in true and eternal life." When the holy Theotokos heard these words, she was filled with joy and gave the angel the same answer as before: *Behold the maidservant of the Lord! Let it be to me* – this time also – *according to your word* (Lk. 1:38). And then the angel left her.

Then the most blessed and glorious Mary the Mother of God arose and went with joy to the Mount of Olives to express her thanksgiving to the Lord in quietness and her petitions concerning herself and the whole world. When she had climbed the mountain, she lifted up her hands and offered up her *reasonable service* (cf. Rom. 12:1) to her Son, her requests and gratitude. Then a great wonder took place, which those who have been granted to experience the like are familiar with and have relayed to us. While she was praying and entreating the Lord in true mystical raptures, all the trees on the mountainside knelt down to the earth and worshipped. When she had finished her petition and thanksgiving, she returned to Zion filled with God.

At once the Lord sent the John the Evangelist and Theologian to her on a cloud, for the holy Virgin greatly desired to see him, since the Lord had bound them together by adoption. And so when the most blessed of women saw him she rejoiced even more and asked to pray together. After they had finished, the holy Queen and eternal virgin told John and the virgins who were with them the latest message from the archangel concerning her translation and showed him the palm branch that she had received from him. She instructed them to put her house in order, to light the lamps, and to burn incense, for she had already arranged it as a bridal chamber in anticipation of the immortal Bridegroom, her most blessed Son, whom she was awaiting with eager expectation. When all was ready, she told her companions and friends the impending mystery of her translation. They at once gathered around her weeping and mourning at her departure, for she had been their hope and help, second only to God.

But their sister, the Mother of God and Queen, comforted them separately, one by one and all together, and addressed a stirring farewell to them: "Be glad, my blessed children, and do not make my translation a cause for mourning, but rather rejoice that the eternal gladness is coming, my Lord and Son, and His grace and mercy will be with you forever."

Then she looked on John the Evangelist and told him to give her garment and veil to the two widows who ministered to her; then she revealed to them the mystery of her departure and the divine visitation she had received concerning this, as well as the meaning of each of these things. Finally, she set the affairs of her funeral in order and instructed them how to anoint her with myrrh and where to bury her spotless body.

When this was done, the glorious Mother of God lay down on a cot, the same bed she washed every night with tears of love for her

Son Jesus Christ and brightened with her prayers and petitions. She then asked them to light the lamps once more.

The believers who were gathered there, apprehending that the hour was near for their mother the most holy Virgin, dissolved into laments. They fell to the ground and begged her not to *leave them orphans* (cf. Jn. 14:18). But if she truly must leave this world, that she would continue to be with them by her grace and intercession.

Then the holy Theotokos opened her exceedingly pure and undefiled mouth and said to them: "The good pleasure of my God and Son is upon me. *This is my God and I will glorify Him; my father's God, and I will exalt Him* (Ex. 15:2). He is my Son, to whom I gave birth according to the flesh, just as His father is God, who is also Creator of His mother. This is why I desire to go to be with Him who gives life and existence to all. But while I am going to be with Him, I will not cease to entreat and intercede on your behalf and on behalf of all Christians and all the world; I will ask the loving Creator by His great mercy to have compassion on all the faithful, to strengthen them and lead them in the path of true life; to turn the unbelievers and gather them all together into a single flock (cf. Jn. 10:16). For He is the good Shepherd, and He gave His life for His sheep and knows them and is known by them (cf. 1 Cor. 13:12)."

And as the most blessed Mother of Christ spoke these words and blessed them, there suddenly came a loud clap of thunder and a cloud borne by a gentle breeze. And out of this great cloud there started to descend to earth the holy and glorious disciples and Apostles of Christ the Savior like drops of myrrh-scented dew, congregating together from the corners of the earth into the courtyard of Mary, the most holy Virgin and Theotokos. At once, John the Evangelist and Theologian received them with a quiet greeting and led them into the presence of the most holy and blessed Virgin. Not only the Twelve had come, but many others of the numerous disciples that had been selected and found worthy of the apostolic succession, as the great Dionysius the Areopagite tells us in his letter to Timothy. He says that he himself, Dionysius, was together with Timothy, Hierotheus, and their other close friends who came there with the Apostles for the departure of the Queen. And so they came and stood before her and venerated her with awe and utmost reverence.

The blessed and most holy Virgin blessed them in turn and announced to them that she would leave this world. She furthermore explained to them about the good news she had received from the archangel concerning her dormition, and once she had shown them the palm branch the leader of the angelic hosts had given her as a symbol of victory and her translation, she comforted them and blessed them again, encouraging and strengthening them to fulfil the preaching of the gospel. She bade farewell to Peter and Paul, as well as all the others, saying: "Rejoice my children, friends and disciples of my God and Son. You are blessed, for you have been found worthy to become disciples of the blessed and glorious Lord and Master who has entrusted to you the ministry of such great mysteries. He has chosen you to participate in His persecutions and sufferings, that He may make you worthy to share also in His glory and kingdom, just as He promised you and orchestrated Himself, the King of glory." She expounded to them such a blessed teaching, befitting the stature of her glory, and once she had put the final affairs of her funeral and burial in order, she raised her hands toward heaven and began to thank the Lord, saying:

"I praise You, King of all and only-begotten Son of the eternal Father, true God of true God, for You have seen fit by the Father's good will and Your ineffable loving-kindness to receive flesh from me Your servant, by the agency of the Holy Spirit.

"I praise You, Giver of every blessing and Bestower of light, the Cause of every good thing and Prince of peace, who has given us grace to know You and the eternal Father and the co-eternal and life-giving Spirit.

"I praise You, for You have been pleased to dwell in my womb, a miracle beyond words.

"I praise You, for You have loved human nature even to the point of suffering death on a cross for our sake, and by Your resurrection You have resurrected our nature from the bowels of Hades, in order to draw it up to heaven and glorify it with inconceivable glory.

"I praise You and magnify Your words, for You have given them to us in all truth; and I believe that all the promises You have made to me will be fulfilled."

When the holy and most blessed Theotokos had finished her hymn and prayer, the holy Apostles were moved by the Holy Spirit and began to speak, to sing praise and glory, such as everyone was able and divinely enlightened. They extolled and praised the incomparable generosity of God's sovereignty, and their wondrous and holy words gladdened the heart of the glorious Mother of God, as the aforementioned Dionysius tells us in the same chapter where he shows the power of the prayers and holy words that the blessed and pious Hierotheus spoke. Likewise, in the same chapter of his writing to Timothy, he mentions the congregation of the holy Apostles at the time of the most holy Theotokos' departure, as well as the way in which each, by the inspiration of the Holy Spirit, uttered words in praise of the almighty power and love of our God and Savior Jesus Christ; for He was pleased to come down to the earth without leaving the bosom of the Father and take on flesh from the immaculate Virgin. He inclined the heavens and descended, for He found the most holy and glorious Mary obedient and exalted above all creation; He desired to indwell her and be clothed by her in the nature of man. And in this way He showed His mercy and saved the human race by His great and ineffable plan of salvation, rendering us rich and glorious by His grace, because of His great mercy and patience.

Consider what the blessed Dionysius himself writes: "I will now tell you all the words of God that our holy disciples and high priests said, though they are truly indescribable, as you yourself know, brother Timothy. I will also tell what the blessed Hierotheus said to the great Apostles, by the grace of the Holy Spirit. He was the wise disciple of the great Paul, and a celebrant of Christ our God, writer of hymns and praises to our immaculate and most blessed mother, as the Apostles and theologians themselves confirmed: 'The Holy Spirit opened his mouth and illumined him to utter such glorifying hymns.'"

After that, the holy Virgin blessed them once more, and her heart was filled with comfort.

And behold! There came Christ her Son and God, glorious and wondrous to behold, flanked by countless hosts of angels, archangels, and beings of other orders: Seraphs, Cherubs, and Thrones. All the angels stood before the Lord with fear, for "where the presence of the king is, there the hosts will also be".

The most holy Theotokos knew all these things in advance and looked forward to them with unshakeable hope. This is why she said, "I believe that all the promises You have made to me will be fulfilled." But then the holy Apostles saw clearly as well and looked in awe upon His divine glory, each as he was able. The Lord had come this time with greater and more awesome majesty than before, for now he appeared brighter than lightning, and even brighter than His transfiguration on Mount Tabor, when He displayed His otherworldly glory, for the risen Christ cannot be approached or beheld.

In the face of such a mystery, *the disciples fell on their faces and were terrified, and became like dead men* (cf. Mt. 17:6). Then the Lord said: *Peace be with you,* as He had before, *when the doors were shut where the disciples were assembled, for fear of the Jews* (Jn. 20:19), in that very same house of John. And now something similar was happening for the dormition of the mother of the risen Lord. When the Apostles heard His voice, more dear to them and coveted than anything else, they took new life and strength in body and soul. They kept watching the resplendent beauty and radiance of His face. Then the most holy, immaculate, and blessed Theotokos was filled with joy, and her face shone with divine brilliance. And she magnified the Godhead even more and prayed for the Apostles and all who were present, gazing with awe and fear on the glory and light that her Son and King Jesus Christ shone forth. And in these last moments, she interceded for the faithful everywhere, praying for the whole world and every soul that calls upon the name of the Lord and His mother, and seeking that wherever these two names are mentioned the riches of divine blessing be poured out.

Then the holy Virgin Mary looked again at her Son and saw such glory that no tongue of man could ever express. And she said: "Bless me, Lord, with Your right hand, and bless all who glorify and remember Your name whenever they offer their prayer and petition to You." Then the Lord stretched out His right hand and blessed His mother, saying: "O blessed Mary, let your heart rejoice, blessed among women, for you have been granted fullness of grace and all gifts from My Father in heaven; and every soul that calls on My name with reverence I shall in no wise overlook, but they shall find mercy and consolation both in this life and in the age to come. And as for you, go in peace and joy to the heavenly dwelling places, unto the infinite treasures of My Father, that you may see My glory and rejoice in the grace of the Holy Spirit."

And at the Lord's command, the angels at once struck up a sweet and gentle hymn in rich and melodious harmony, while the holy Apostles bowed their heads in reverence before the revelations of the Holy Spirit; and one by one they offered an angelic song to the Virgin. And with that, the most holy Mother of the Lord delivered her blessed and immaculate soul to her Son and King and fell into a sweet and gentle sleep. Just as she had inexplicably given birth to the Lord Jesus without pain, so also at her dormition she was spared the throes of death, for the King and Creator of every being's nature – He Himself has and does transform the laws of nature.

The angelic hosts raised their hands in astonishment as her most holy soul sped away. An ineffable fragrance filled the house of Zion and all the surrounding area (cf. Jn. 12:3). A bright essence floated above her immaculate body, invisible to physical eyes. And so the Teacher and the disciples, the heavens and the earth, were both present together with the Virgin. And the blessed Lord and glorious Master of all led the holy soul of His immaculate mother into the heavens, while the disciples laid her spotless body to rest in the earth, that they might anoint it with aloes and take it at last to the place she had desired. From there she would shortly be translated into paradise or wherever her Son and God desired.

The holy Apostles then bore out the bed upon which was laid the body of the Mother of God, more perfect than the vault of heaven. They honored it with hymns and spiritual songs, they embraced it with fear and trembling, showing not only their faith and devotion, but also their assurance of receiving grace and great succor (if, of course, their faith was accompanied by commensurate works).

Meanwhile, as soon as it became known that the Queen of all had taken her leave, those suffering from all manner of sicknesses gathered there. The eyes of the blind were opened miraculously, the deaf found their hearing, the lame learned to walk, the demon-possessed were made clean, and every malady and affliction was healed. The skies and the highest heavens were purified by the most holy soul passing through them, and the earth was honored and blessed to receive the immaculate body that had received God Himself.

The Apostles then urged the blessed Peter to utter the funeral prayer; Peter however appointed Paul and John to offer up this prayer. But they would not comply but bowed before him as the chief of all the company of Apostles. Then the blessed Peter in turn gave way to their insistence, as befitted the present mystery. And once he had finished praying, they swathed and anointed with oil the body that had contained the Uncontainable, the King and Creator of things visible and invisible, and laid it to rest on the holy bed. At once the blessed Peter struck up a new hymn, and all joined in, the choir of the Apostles answering in antiphonies with the hosts of heaven singing invisibly along with them. The very air was filled with their bright beams and smelled of incense.

Then the holy Apostles lifted the hallowed bed upon their shoulders and made for Gethsemane, under the guidance of the Holy Spirit, as the most holy Theotokos herself had arranged beforehand. The angels led the way as escorts, and others followed after her holy remains and her attendants. The funeral of the most blessed and glorified Theotokos was stunning and most holy, for the Apostles sang psalms while all the faithful entreated the temple of the Savior with faith.

All those who were sick and suffering from various diseases were not only *sixty mighty ones about the bed of the King* (cf. Song 3:7), as the Scripture says, but the visible multitude of the Apostles with the mighty company of all believers, and the countless invisible hosts of angels.

And yet even so the enemy of the truth did not hesitate to show his audacity. He stirred up the Jews once again to murder and rage; for when they saw the brilliant company of the most glorified Mother of God with the multitude of the Apostles and the believers following her, as well as the countless miracles that the grace of the Queen of all had brought to past, and when they heard the divine hymns, they were seized with jealous rage – *the foolish and thoughtless people* [...] *in whom is no understanding* (Deut. 32:6, 28). Just as when the multitude of innocent children had accompanied Christ the King of all with palm branches and shouts of "*Hosanna, blessed is He who comes in the name of the Lord, the King of Israel!*" (Jn. 12:13; Mt. 21:9), the unholy chief priests and scribes had opposed the Giver of every good thing in their rage and wicked envy, even condemning Him to death, and death on a cross; so now also at the funeral of His glorious and immaculate mother they strove to disturb the peace and the deep reverence of the procession of the Apostles and believers, trying to break that holy congress with wild shouts.

Then one of those wicked men, more carnal than the others, fierce and murderous, rushed menacingly at the congregation of Christians who were accompanying the *ark of holiness* (cf. Ps. 131:8). He waited at first until the holy Apostles had approached, bearing the heavenly treasure, the container of the uncontainable and uncircumscribable nature, then he opened his vile hands and violently seized the bed whereon was laid the most holy remains of the most blessed Queen, before which even the angels trembled, and the Cherubs looked on with utmost reverence. The calloused oaf took hold of this wooden bed and tried with all his might to turn it over. O what a bestial soul! O what a frenzied reason! But he received at once the just reward for his crime. Indeed, that very instant the arms that had seized that holy bed were struck from his shoulders, for he had dared to touch that which was unlawful to approach or even gaze upon (cf. 2 Kgd. 6). The wrath of God fell on him, and he dissolved into cries and shrieks. He and all the Jews with him were seized with horror and despair, for the divine sentence had fallen over them and the fury of a wrathful angel. They fell back at once in a fright, with the angel of the Lord in pursuit. This miracle took place in order to throw the Jews into confusion and fear, but also to give the believers greater cause for boasting and glory. The one who had been seized with such fury and had been counted among the foes and mockers of the Lord, once he had been punished for his misdeed, was filled with shame and came to his senses and exchanged his former derision for faith, and his evil for fear and contrition; in the same way he traded his slanders and insults for repentance and supplication. He had no hands to raise in petition, but with hot tears and a baleful voice he called to the most holy Virgin and pled her mercy.

And so the cause of all this became also the cause of jubilation to all. She saw fit not to strike the guilty man with eternal torment, sorrow, mourning, and punishment, but merely a temporary deformity of the body. But she healed the incurable wounds of his soul, and even his fellow aggressors were found worthy to become Christians and be called children of God, by the grace of baptism. And finally, she in her great mercy also healed his hands. Once the Hebrew had been punished and recognized his error, he swiftly repented and prayed with hot tears, calling fervently on the name of Christ and His most holy mother Mary. The holy Apostle Peter ordered them to halt the holy procession and turn to the Mother of God with prayers and petitions. So they brought before her the guilty man, now contrite and repentant, with blood gushing from his arms and tears from his eyes. He approached the holy bed; not as he had just before, but rather with supplications in fear and trembling. The blessed Peter held his mutilated limbs in place, and at once, by the grace of Christ and His most holy mother, the arms that were dangling from his shoulders were joined to the rest of his body; and not only did the awful pain and agony cease, but even the marks left by the wounds were nowhere to be seen. And so the man believed in Christ, was baptized, and was counted among the faithful, giving glory to the Lord and His most holy and glorious mother. This miracle, the sudden injury and instant healing, strengthened the faith of the many doubters and converted many of the Jews. They confessed the Lord Jesus Christ as God whom they had crucified and proclaimed His mother to be the Theotokos.

And so after all these things, the Apostles took the bed back onto their holy shoulders, with even more brilliance and heartfelt hymns and praises, for the bed now shone brightly with the grace of the most holy Queen, guarded by heavenly and earthly battalions, invisibly adorned by thousands of angels and archangels, and visibly accompanied by hymns and spiritual songs.

When they reached Gethsemane, they laid the spotless body in the tomb, the holy incarnate throne of the Lord, the true Holy of Holies, the redemption of our nature, the instrument in which the awesome mystery of unification of human and divine nature took place. She is truly the city of God of whom *glorious things are spoken* (cf. Ps. 86:3) from generation to generation, the mountain whereon God was pleased to dwell (cf. Ps. 67:16), the closed gate through which none may enter but God alone, which He has kept shut. The only virgin mother, the only immaculate Theotokos.

And yet it was not strange that the mother of life was laid to rest in a tomb, for her Son also (who is Life and Immortality itself) endured bodily death and burial, that by His death He might put away death and grant life to the world.

But we must not keep silent about the burial of the Virgin's body. When they reached the tomb, they left the bed next to it, on which the priceless treasure had been laid, and were obliged to take the blessed body into their hands and carry it into the tomb. All the holy Apostles and the others who followed were terrified of looking at it and did not dare to touch the holy and most blessed receptacle, for they saw the light with which she was clothed and the divine grace that overshadowed her.

Ultimately, all the Apostles again agreed that Peter and Paul should bury the holy body, for John the Evangelist bore the incense and was burning it as a sweet-smelling offering about the holy body of the Queen, and washing it with his tears. So Peter and Paul took hold, not of the hallowed body, but of some strips of cloth hanging from it, and lifted it up off the bed with utmost reverence and care, and placed it in the tomb. And so these brilliant and incomparable Apostles, who had once duly and fittingly honored and served her Son, now also served His mother, who is honored by angels and men, called blessed by all generations, as the blessed one herself had foretold (cf. Lk. 1:48). Thus, when this holy, most holy body of the most blessed Theotokos and eternal Virgin Mary had been laid in the tomb, the holy Apostles remained there for three days, basking in the beautiful song of the holy angels, a lovely and enchanting psalmody which no mortal tongue can describe, as David the prophet says: *I will go into the place of Your wondrous tabernacle, unto the house of God with a voice of jubilation and confession and the sound of celebration* (Ps. 41:5). Truly she is the 'wondrous tabernacle', the 'house of God' in which He Himself is pleased to dwell, the Lord of glory and the King of peace.

This story has been handed down by true and reliable witnesses, who passed it on to the following generations. And it is certain and sure that, while all the holy Apostles were gathered at the funeral of the Queen, one of them had not been informed in time as the others had been. The rest were waiting for him to share as well in the blessing that they themselves had received from the grace-giving and blessed body. And so on the third day, this Apostle found the other brothers singing before the holy tomb. He himself also heard the dulcet harmonies of the angels and implored the holy Apostles to open the hallowed grave that he also might worship the body of the most holy Theotokos, that which had received God. The blessed Apostles complied with the brother's request under the guidance of the Holy Spirit and opened the grave with reverence. But when they removed the stone, they did not find the glorious body of the Theotokos, for it had been translated to the place her Son and God had seen fit. In fact, when He suffered death for the sake of our salvation, he deigned to be laid in a tomb and rise again from there on the third day, and in the same way He saw fit to lay the body of His most holy mother in a tomb, and then after three days, according to His will, to translate her into eternal immortality and once more be united with her soul. This unique honor was reserved by the Creator of all things for the mother who had given birth to Him, as He alone knows how, the King of glory and the Lord over life and death.

O grave! You were found empty! The strips of linen in which she was wrapped were found within, but the body of the Virgin was not. She had been raptured away to her Son and God, that she might live and reign with Him in body and soul. And so the human nature was made worthy of exaltation into the eternal kingdom, not only because of her Son, but also because of His mother.

The blessed Apostles were dumbfounded at this; they rejoiced and asserted that the absence of the last Apostle had been the work of divine providence, that this great mystery might be revealed. That the grave might be opened because of him and all might see the translation of the holy body. And so they glorified Christ in the presence of such a great miracle, for He had seen fit to honor His most holy and immaculate mother. Indeed, everything was bathed in light and a sweet odor, which wafted out of the holy tomb within which the body of the holy Virgin had been laid, more perfect than the heavens. Both the scent and the light had gone out into all of Gethsemane. So they shut that holy grave again, and news of the glorious translation of the most holy Theotokos spread like wildfire to the ends of the earth.

Moreover, an old account has come down to us that the Apostle who came on the third day was Thomas, and he came from India. And so, just as Thomas had served to corroborate the resurrection of the Lord, when the Lord entered through *locked doors* (Jn. 20:19, 26) on the eighth day and showed him His wounds and His holy side; so also now Thomas served to spread the news of the translation of the incorrupt and spotless body of the holy and glorified Theotokos and eternal Virgin Mary.

Whereupon the holy Apostles, when they had prayed together and said farewell, went their separate ways again, each back to the country he had been appointed, to preach the gospel and *make disciples of all nations* (Mt. 28:19), just as they had been commanded by the Lord; they went in His power and aided by His miracles. And so the heavens and the angelic hosts were complete, now that the soul and ultimately the body of the most holy and blessed Virgin had made its ascent. But even the earth was sanctified by her life in it, including her burial and even the holy garments of her body. And so the skies and all of creation was blessed by her piety and constant good works. And even every city and nation and the souls of all the faithful are filled with her ceaseless wonderworking activities, her healings and the countless blessings that the Mother of God bestows on each. In fact, who can tell how much help and intercession she gives to each of us, and what tongue can fully express the riches of her bounties?

IX: THE DEPOSITION OF THE HOLY ROBE

It is good for us to include in our narrative the manner in which Mary bestowed her incorrupt robe as a sacred heirloom upon the city of Constantine, how the nation of the faithful saw it as a great boon, and how the immaculate Virgin bequeathed it as an inviolable treasure to the Church. Unto the glory of Christ our God and the praise of the most holy eternal Virgin, His mother, our only hope and mediator.

In the days of the faithful King of the Greeks Leon the Great, who was king after Marcian, there lived two patricians: the one was named Galbius and the other Candidus. They were brothers by blood, but also brothers in magnanimity. They were adorned with every manner of good works, lacking but one: the pinnacle of all virtues, true faith. They were found wanting, for they had been caught in the net of the Arian heresy. They were of the house of Aspar and Ardaburius, which in those days held great sway in the Capital. But God had forgiven them fully for this sin, for even though they supported the heresy of Arius, divine grace did not let them end in destruction, because of their good works. Rather, it turned them from wickedness to truth, so that they became not only a bulwark of the Orthodox faith, but even went on to instruct many others in virtue and lead them to salvation, even though they had been used to living in delusion. So when they turned to Orthodoxy, they took advantage of even more opportunities for good works and charity to the poor, that they might please the Lord in all things. And so the most holy and immaculate Mother of God, when she saw fit to bestow some of her incorrupt vestments on her own city, used the providence of these godly men. And this is how it came to pass.

There awakened in the patricians a fervent desire to journey to Jerusalem on pilgrimage to the Holy Land. They communicated this to the Emperor Leon and the Empress Verina, and with their leave they set out, taking with them many servants and friends, as well as a great multitude of soldiers. They traveled through Palestine, just the two of them alone, and eventually took the road leading to Galilee, for they wished to see Nazareth and Capernaum. By the time they had reached the vicinity, night had fallen, and they had to search for a place to sleep. And the providence of God saw fit that they should stay in a small village. Now, in this village there were many people, and one of them was an old maid who, though a true Israelite by law, showed by her deeds a deep piety. Truly, her soul was a dark land, but it had already been made ready for the light of divine knowledge. This aged woman held the treasure of the holy robe of the glorious Mother of Christ. And so led by divine providence, Galbius and Candidus stayed at her house. When they had sat down to dinner, they noticed that in the innermost part of the house there was another chamber, lit with many lamps. It was also filled with sweet-smelling incense, and a number of sick men lay on the floor. So naturally, they assumed that something holy was inside and were burning with curiosity about what it could be. So they went and called the mistress of the house to dine with them, that they might ask her about the matter. But she refused to come, citing the precept of the Law that did not allow the Jews to break bread with Christians. But they convinced her to come to them and managed to reassure her saying: "Bring with you the food you have prepared and eat it later. Simply sit and speak with us. There is no harm in that."

Finally, the woman acquiesced to the two lordly pilgrims and came and sat and conversed with them. When they had spoken at length, they asked her to tell them what exactly was in the inmost chamber of the house. They had surmised that it had something to do with the Old Testament.

Meanwhile, the woman preferred to describe the circumstances only, without mentioning what it was. So she said: "Do you see all these sick men, my lords? God has so willed that in this place demons are cast out, the blind receive their sight, the lame walk, the deaf hear, and all maladies are cured."

Now, the lordly pilgrims realized that something great was afoot, and they asked her all the more urgently: "And what is the cause of so many miracles? Tell us."

She replied: "An ancient tradition that has been handed down to us tells that God appeared to one of the Patriarchs in this place, and that is why it is so full of grace."

When the Greeks heard this, they pondered whether her answer was sincere. At length, they asked her again to tell them the whole truth: "This is the reason we have taken upon us so much hardship and such a long journey – our desire to visit the Holy Land as pilgrims."

She answered them yet again: "That is all I know."

But the two pilgrims realized that she did not want to reveal to them the whole truth, for the Queen of all wished to bless the Byzantines with the great treasure and told them in their hearts that this was not the truth. And so they begged her even more fervently to tell them the secret, and swore terrible oaths to convince her that they were in earnest and get her to tell them the whole truth. So finally she spoke what had been hidden in her heart, with her eyes downcast in shame and tears welling up in her eyes. And this is what she said:

"O men, I have never divulged this secret to anyone until now. For my parents bequeathed to me, their only daughter, the chest with an oath, but did not tell me what was inside. One of my relatives, a maiden, had instructed them to reveal it to another maiden, once she had died. O venerable patricians, I am that maiden. And I have kept until now the treasure of that woman of my family who remained a virgin. And now there is no other consecrated virgin like myself left to whom I can pass it on, as it has been passed on until now. This is why I am revealing this matter to you. You must keep this treasure in trust.

"This box contains the robe of Mary the Theotokos. Indeed, we have been told by our great-grandfathers that before her dormition, the Mother of God left her two garments to two virgins who served her. One of them was my ancestor. This elder took the venerable robe, stored in a small box, and left it to be guarded from generation to generation. She gave orders that whoever guards the box must be a virgin. And now the box sits in the inmost chamber of this house and contains this garment of the eternal Virgin, the Mother of God; and from it the miracles flow forth. This is the whole truth on this matter, my august princes, and no one here in Israel has known this until now."

The splendid patricians were dumbfounded at the revelation of the mystery concerning the holy treasure, and their hearts were filled with joy, but also fear. They knelt before the woman and said:

"Be assured that no one in Jerusalem will hear this testimony from us. But you will have the special protection of the Lady Theotokos if you let us spend the night in the room where this holy treasure is kept."

The woman consented, and the two men went into the inner chamber, and *did not give sleep to their eyes nor slumber to their eyelids* (Ps. 131:4), but spent the whole night in prayer and supplication, thanking God for this great mystery He had entrusted to them. When they saw that all the sick men had fallen asleep, the took the exact measurements of the box in which the precious treasure was kept and faithfully recorded its structure and composition. They awoke early in the morning and took their leave of the woman, saying:

"If you need anything from Jerusalem, tell us, for we will pass by here on our way back."

She replied: "I have no need of anything, except the assurance that I will see you again in peace."

Galbius and Candidus went to Jerusalem and fulfilled all that they had promised to the Lord, worshipped at the most holy places and gave generously to the poor, to monasteries, and to churches. Meanwhile, during their stay there, they hired a craftsman and discretely instructed him to build them a box to the exact specifications and the same shape, out of old planks. The craftsman constructed it as they had described. They also prepared a magnificent golden cloth to cover the box, and once they had finished worshipping at the holy places and monasteries, they took the prayers of all the fathers and the blessing of the patriarch as provisions and set off along the same road by which they had come. They now had with them the box they had made, and once they reached that village, they rejoiced to stay again at the aged maiden's house. They offered her lamps, much incense, and exotic spices. The woman received the courtiers as old friends.

They then asked to spend another night in the chamber where the treasure of grace was kept, and she consented easily. So they went in there with full confidence and devoted that night to thanksgiving and supplication to God. They spoke to the holy Mother of God with hot tears: "We, your servants, know, O glorious Lady, what happened to Uzzah when he laid hands on the ark of the covenant (cf. 2 Kgd. 6:6-7). So how should we who are guilty of countless misdeeds dare to approach this ark, within which just such a great treasure is kept? How should we stretch out our hands to it, if you do not give us your leave? And so we ask you, we beg you to engender this desire in our hearts, for us to take this treasure to the city where your name is most honored, that it might be an eternal ward and protective bulwark to it." They prayed to the Mother of God all through the night, and when morning came they were filled with such compunction by her grace, that they were convinced she had heard their prayer. So they drew near to the holy ark with fear and trembling, when all those who were present had fallen asleep. They took the box and secured their holy treasure, assisted by divine grace. And in its place they set the box they had made in its likeness in Jerusalem, and covered it with the gilded cloth they had made. Early in the morning they bade the woman farewell in peace and showed her the beautiful cloth they had consecrated to the most holy Virgin. This pleased her immensely, and she promised that she would leave it there forever. And so they gave some money to all the sick and lame beggars and set out joyfully on their way home.

Now, once they reached Constantinople, the ancient city of Byzas, they did not want the Emperor or the Patriarch to learn of this great thing, for they feared that the King would not show the priceless treasure the honor it was due, and so they hid this great blessing. And so they sought to keep the pearl of great price hidden in obscurity, by the help of the most holy Mother of God.

They owned property next to the outer walls by the sea, where they themselves also lived. The place was called Blachernae. There they built a church and were careful to avoid revealing their secret at all costs, and so they even dedicated the church to the Apostles Peter and Mark. Inside they placed the great treasure and took care that the holy sanctuary where it was kept be ministered to with unceasing psalmody and that there be sweet-smelling incense kept burning there at all times and it be lit with lamps and undying candles. These were the measures they took to honor the holy robe. And for a long time, the secret remained hidden.

But the most holy Lady, the hope and intercessor of all the faithful, was not pleased that such a great boon be restricted to only two patricians, and that this common blessing for all be kept in obscurity and they alone benefit from it. And so she spoke to the hearts of the honored patricians and told them that they must reveal their hidden secret. And so they went to the faithful Emperor Leon and told him the great thing, explaining how the priceless treasure had reached the Capital. When the faithful king heard all these things, he rejoiced greatly. He immediately revealed the hidden treasure, and the blessed Galbius and Candidus, who had accomplished this holy service, were honored above all others. Then the king and servant of God Leon and the most faithful Queen Verina built a magnificent church on the spot, funded by the royal coffers, and ordered a larnax made of gold and silver to be built to house the holy treasure. They decorated the church with gifts and numerous donations to their eternal memory. King Leon and Verina finished out the days of their rule in prosperity and virtue and entered into everlasting life and the eternal kingdom. In the same way, Galbius and Candidus, the faithful and true servants of the most holy Theotokos died in faith and service to the Lord. And the box of the mystery remained as an eternal treasure in the faithful church and the city that worshipped the true God. This ark did not contain Moses' tablets written by God's hand, but they kept the precious robe of the glorified and most blessed Theotokos, with which she had clothed her spotless and immaculate body, and also wrapped Christ our God, from the moment of His incarnation and birth to the moment of our salvation. And many times after that she had covered him as a nursing babe, as is done with all people of that age. Whom did she nurse and cover? Him who is true life, who brings all flesh into the world. She is the reason why this garment of the immaculate and glorified Mother of God has remained intact even unto our days. And in a similar way the spotless and most holy Mother of Christ gave to her city her holy life as well, which had wrapped the body that contained the Uncontainable, the King of all. And that is why a second church was built by the faithful kings, even more stunning, to the glory of the holy Mother of God. This church is called Chalkoprateia, and it houses the incorrupt girdle, as a crown of glory and unshakeable bastion of the city, a guarantee of victory to the kings who serve God.

Manufactured by Amazon.ca
Bolton, ON